STRUCTURED DESIGN USING HIPO-II

William H. Roetzheim

PRENTICE HALL, Englewood Cliffs, New Jersey 07632

Roetzheim, William H.
    Structured design using HIPO-II / William H. Roetzheim.
        p.   cm.
    Bibliography: p.
    Includes index.
    ISBN 0-13-853599-X
    1. System design. 2. HIPO technique. 3. Electronic data
processing--Structured techniques.   I. Title.
    QA76.9.S88R64   1990
    005.1--dc19   89-3709

REF
QA
76.9
.S88
R64
1990

Editorial/production supervision
and interior design: Karen Bernhaut
Cover design: 20/20 Services, Inc.
Manufacturing buyer: Mary Ann Gloriande

© 1990 by Prentice-Hall, Inc.
A division of Simon & Schuster
Englewood Cliffs, New Jersey 07632

The publisher offers discounts on this book when ordered
in bulk quantities. For more information, write:

Special Sales/College Marketing
Prentice-Hall, Inc.
College Technical and Reference Division
Englewood Cliffs, NJ 07632

Structured Designer's Toolbox and SDT are trademarks of William H. Roetzheim & Associates.
IBM PC is a trademark of International Business Machines Corporation.

Printed in the United States of America

10 9 8 7 6 5 4 3 2 1

ISBN 0-13-853599-X

Prentice-Hall International (UK) Limited, *London*
Prentice-Hall of Australia Pty. Limited, *Sydney*
Prentice-Hall Canada Inc., *Toronto*
Prentice-Hall Hispanoamericana, S.A., *Mexico*
Prentice-Hall of India Private Limited, *New Delhi*
Prentice-Hall of Japan, Inc., *Tokyo*
Simon & Schuster Asia Pte. Ltd., *Singapore*
Editora Prentice-Hall do Brasil, Ltda., *Rio de Janeiro*

To my third child, Regina,
whose bright eyes and cheerful smile
brighten the lives of all who are around her,

and to my wife, Marianne,
who grows lovelier both inside and out
with every passing day.

CONTENTS

PREFACE

Much of the software development world seems to have fallen in love with the concepts of data flow and entity relationship diagrams (the Yourdon/Constantine/DeMarco approach to software design). While I agree that these concepts are valuable tools, I wonder if they are as universally applicable as many CASE vendors would have us believe. They certainly seem to be well suited to developing large data base-intensive applications, perhaps for the banking industry and probably using COBOL. What about military or scientific applications? What about real time programming? What about applications where the user interface spells the difference between success and failure, including mass market software applications? What about small to mid-sized programs in which the software design changes often and the systems analysts don't have the time to learn a complex new technique? I believe that an alternative approach is required, not to replace other techniques, but to complement them. I sought a technique that was easy to learn and use, involved the end user in all aspects of the design, was adaptable to projects with varying sizes and requirements, and facilitated design changes throughout the project. I also felt that the technique should be suitable for CASE implementation on a small microcomputer without requiring expensive high-resolution graphic displays and expensive high-performance CPUs to drive the displays.

I believe that the most easily understood design technique ever developed is HIPO (Hierarchy plus Input-Process-Output). I have used this technique on many surprisingly complex projects with great success, and have found that customers can relate to the HIPO representation of a design. Unfortunately, the original HIPO technique has some serious flaws that have caused it to fall out of favor. This book describes a reborn HIPO, a HIPO that includes program design capabilities that allow HIPO-II to compete with even the most extensive "modern" design technique while still retaining the charm and simplicity of the original technique. If you have had difficulty applying other design methods and CASE tools to your projects, HIPO-II may be just what you needed. If you are looking for a method of implementing formal design and CASE in your programming environment with a minimum of expense for training and hardware, HIPO-II is appropriate. If you are already using another design technique, you may still find it worthwhile to add HIPO-II to your "bag of tricks" to be applied to selected problems.

William H. Roetzheim

```
┌──────────┐
│ chapter  │
│    1     │
└──────────┘
```

STRUCTURED DESIGN
in the
REAL WORLD

This book **is not** about producing better software designs. Software design efforts manufacture products that do not have any intrinsic value whatsoever. In the real world, software design is a means to an end, and nothing more. Effective software design must contribute to the real task at hand—the development of working software. Software design efforts must help to reduce software costs, development risk, and implementation time. Software design efforts must improve the value of the software as perceived through the eyes of the end user. Software design efforts must improve the long-term satisfaction of the customer, resulting in follow-on work.

This book **does** introduce a new software design technique that integrates software design products with the following:

- Project management requirements for control of the project
- User requirements for prototyping
- Programmer requirements for clarity, consistency, and convenience
- Systems analyst requirements for flexibility and power

This design technique, called *HIPO-II* (Hierarchy plus Input-Process-Output-II), is built upon a foundation of one of the simplest hierarchical design techniques in use, HIPO.

In this chapter, we will describe the components of structured software development, and introduce some problems with traditional structured design approaches. We will describe briefly the evolution of structured development, and introduce HIPO as originally developed by IBM. Finally, we will introduce HIPO-II, an updated version of HIPO which corrects problems with the original technique and adds many new features.

1.1 COMPONENTS OF STRUCTURED SOFTWARE DEVELOPMENT

As shown in Fig. 1.1, structured software development consists of the following components:

- *Structured Project Management*—managing software development efforts

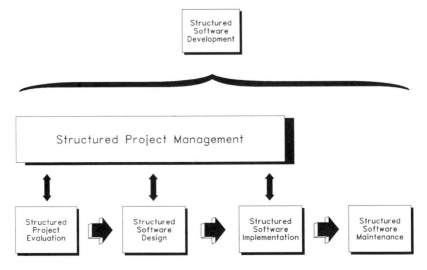

Figure 1.1   Components of Structured Software Development

- *Structured Project Evaluation*—estimating the value of a software development project to your company. This component includes approaches to estimating development cost, risk, return on investment, cash flow, etc.
- *Structured Software Design*—designing computer software
- *Structured Software Implementation*—coding, integrating, and testing computer software
- *Structured Software Maintenance*—maintaining and enhancing existing computer software

Notice that we do not include an *analysis* activity. Problem analysis is treated as a precursor to the software development process. This is consistent with typical government projects for which the government completes the problem analysis prior to writing the Request for Proposal (RFP) and hiring a contractor.

The difference between a structured and an unstructured approach to any of these software development components is that the structured approach is

1. **Consistent:** The approach will give predictable results for a wide range of projects, when used by a broad cross section of individuals, under a variety of specific circumstances.

2. **Logical:** The approach is based on theories, heuristics, and algorithms that make sense logically and have been validated in practice.

3. **Teachable:** The approach must involve step-by-step, quantitative actions that can be taught to individuals with a wide range of previous experience.

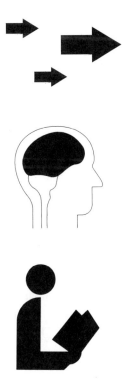

Figure 1.1 showed how these five components are coupled together during the various stages of a software development project. Structured project evaluation is necessary to ensure that the project's technical, schedule, and cost goals can be achieved by *any* design. Structured software design takes a set of goals that are achievable and produces a design which meets these goals. Structured software implementation starts with a workable design and implements working software which can be maintained. Structured project management requires participation during the project evaluation, software designs, and software implementation phases. Many companies spend considerable time, money, and effort implementing one or more component(s) of structured software development, only to find that the neglected component(s) became the weak link in the development chain. *Each* of these components must be implemented to ensure consistent success in your software development efforts.

1.2 COMPONENTS OF EFFECTIVE DESIGN

One common problem with traditional software design techniques is that they are engineered exclusively around the requirements of the systems analyst. Although it is true that the systems analyst normally will be the primary software designer, the representation of the design has far-reaching consequences for other project participants. Software design has a significant effect on four distinct groups of individuals, all of which must approve of and benefit from the design approach used by the systems analyst. Structured design is important to

- Project Managers (the managers)
- End Users (the customer)
- Programmers (the implementors)
- Systems Analysts (the designers)

Figure 1.2 summarizes some of the more important design characteristics as viewed through the eyes of each project participant. Let's look at some criteria each group might use when deciding if a design approach is acceptable.

Figure 1.2   Multiple Perspectives When Evaluating Design Techniques

Project Managers

Project managers are concerned with customer satisfaction, project cost and risk, and task scheduling. Some specific questions of primary importance to the project manager are likely to be:

- Does the design method break the project down hierarchically into specific work packages (modules)? These work packages should involve well-defined interfaces to allow concurrent development and be sufficiently clear that task completion can be verified. These work packages will form the basis of the project schedule, specific work assignments, cost estimates, risk estimates, and other details of the project plan.
- Will the design method facilitate communication between the systems analyst, the programmers, the project manager, and the end users to ensure that the software that is implemented is satisfactory to all participants?
- Is the design method easy to learn, allowing new members of the project team to become productive quickly?
- Are the design outputs sufficiently clear and detailed to allow verification and validation (testing) during development?

To better understand the expectations of the project manager, refer to my book *Structured Computer Project Management* (Prentice Hall, 1988).

End Users

End users want to be active members of the design team, and expect the design method to facilitate this interaction. The design documentation should be clear and nonintimidating to end users with little or no technical training. End users should feel comfortable reviewing the design, identifying problems, suggesting corrections, and sketching out requirements. The proposed user interface should be especially well defined during the design process, often involving some degree of prototyping.

Programmers

Programmers are expected to use the design output to implement and test the actual software. Junior members of the programming team may have limited prior exposure to the design technique being used, but they will play a critical role in the ultimate success of the project. The design outputs should be clear and unambiguous to all members of the project team.

I once completed a project design using detailed data flow diagrams (based on a customer's preference). Because the design documents were quite complex, I felt that an introduction to the problem and resulting design was necessary. I wrote a three-page narrative description which summarized the processing performed by various program modules. I was not able to participate in the software implementation effort, but was called back to the project several months later when the finished top level components did not properly integrate. It did not take long to determine that the components causing problems did not even closely match the design as documented in the data flow diagrams. When confronted with this fact, the programmers involved explained that they did not understand the data flow diagrams so they relied on my three-page narrative description to determine what to code!

Systems Analysts

The systems analyst using the selected design technique on a day-to-day basis is concerned with each of the above items, but also must consider factors associated with flexibility, power, and ease of use. Some examples of capabilities most systems analysts would require are as follows:

- The design technique should use graphical techniques that are easy to draw and print, preferably using a standard high-speed printer. This allows design outputs to be produced quickly without requiring expensive plotters or time-consuming artwork.
- The technique should recognize the types of modules the analyst must work with. For example, most software hierarchies consist of menu choices, interrupt modules, keyboard-activated modules, internal processing modules, and common and library modules.
- The design approach should facilitate the quick creation and modification of program designs. It is important that the systems analyst be able to perform ''what if'' type analysis and present alternate design approaches without excessive effort.
- The design technique should be presentable in varying degrees of detail to allow specific subsets of the design to be discussed or examined. This capability greatly simplifies design walkthroughs.

How well do traditional software design techniques meet the needs of these project participants? Unfortunately, the results are not especially impressive. The following section addresses some typical problem areas I have encountered.

1.3 PROBLEMS WITH TRADITIONAL STRUCTURED DESIGN

Should a computer program be developed to the highest possible quality? Should software be carefully designed to be maintainable with minimal effort? Should we ensure that software is efficient? More often than not, the answers are no, no, and no! Software development is a tradeoff between many competing factors (see Fig. 1.3). Developing a word processing program to the same quality requirements used for space shuttle software would probably not be cost effective. Spending time to make a "throw-away" program maintainable would be unwise. Optimizing code for efficiency is often neither necessary nor desirable. The goal of structured software design is to

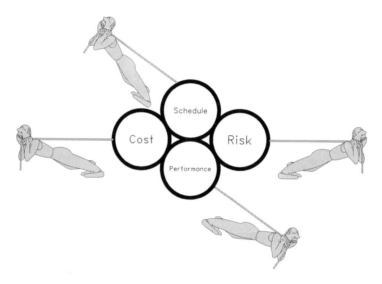

Figure 1.3   Software Development Trade-offs

- Assist project managers in their efforts to estimate costs, allocate and schedule resources, perform cost-benefit trade-offs, and minimize development risk.
- Ensure that the final software meets the needs of the end user. This will normally involve quality, technical, cost, efficiency, and maintainability requirements.
- Help the programming team to effectively implement and test the computer software.

All too often the software design team spends endless months refining the smallest details of the software. In effect, the designers micro-manage the programmers. The end result is a project in which the deadline is reached before a single line of code has been written.

Many traditional structured design techniques fail to recognize that the design is simply a means to an end. They attempt to approach design perfection, at the expense of cost and schedule factors.

Some of the worst software designs I have ever reviewed were delivered in multi-volume sets consisting of thousands of pages of documentation. Some of the best software designs I have seen consisted of several pages of notes and figures on coffee-stained notebook paper. Overdocumentation tends to bury important aspects of the design, stifle change, and discourage effective technical review. The best design possible uses the minimum amount of paper necessary to communicate effectively.

Many traditional structured design techniques encourage drastic overdocumentation, thus increasing development cost and decreasing effective interactions between participants.

Software designs can be represented in a wide variety of ways, including structured or unstructured text, hierarchy charts, and network charts. Many traditional design techniques result in design documentation which is time-consuming (and often expensive) to produce and change. Wall-size data flow diagrams or structure charts are a common example. These monuments to the design team are the most effective deterrent to change possible, stifling the creative feedback mechanism between project participants that is the very lifeblood of successful software development.

Many methods of representing software designs are inherently difficult to modify, thus stifling the iterative process required by all good design efforts.

Many advanced design techniques result in design documentation that may be more complex than the final source code. Professional analysts study and work with the technique for years, gaining proficiency over time. They fail to recognize that

- The programmers required to implement the design are often confused by the format of the design documents, resulting in improper implementations.
- The poor end user is totally intimidated and confused, thus effectively preventing the most valuable member of the project team from contributing at all.

Software design techniques must be completely understandable to even the most junior programmer, and must be readable by end users. Many traditional design techniques cannot pass this simple test.

One of the most common failings of traditional software design techniques is that they look good on small, simple projects, but fall apart on real projects. Real projects involve hundreds or thousands of program modules, not four or five. Real problems involve hundreds or thousands of data flows, not dozens. Real problems may require design representations that primarily stress the algorithms, the data, the user interface, or some combination of these. Traditional techniques that focus on only one of these areas will never handle the full range of projects a software development team is likely to encounter.

1.4 EVOLUTION OF STRUCTURED DEVELOPMENT

Perhaps it is worth taking a minute to review the evolution of structured development. A historical overview (see Fig. 1.4) shows us that software problems, originally perceived as being primarily coding problems, are slowly being recognized as involving all aspects of a project.

Perceived Problem   Solution Approach   Developed Tools

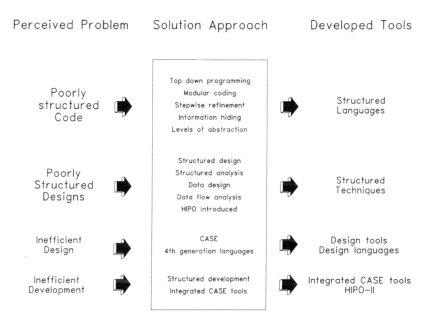

Figure 1.4   Evolution of Structured Development

Early software problems were perceived as being primarily coding and testing problems, so attention focused on these aspects of development. Structured coding conventions became popular with the introduction of concepts such as top-down programming (Mills, 1971), modular coding (Parnas, 1972), and stepwise refinement (Wirth, 1974). Code was made easier to modify and test using the ideas of information hiding (Parnas, 1971) and levels of abstraction (Dijkstra, 1972). Tools centered on new or improved high-level languages designed to facilitate and/or force the implementation of structured coding concepts.

By the mid- to late 1970s, early success in structured coding had solved many of the more obvious code-related problems, only to expose the more serious problems associated with disorganized, unstructured software designs. Effort turned to the design and analysis stage of software development, and a host of new techniques were developed and introduced. Improvements to designing and representing program control flow were primarily extensions of concepts originated earlier in the structured coding areas. The importance of data design and data flow analysis was recognized, and work in this area involved development of new approaches both to analyzing and representing this data. It was at this point that the original HIPO (Hierarchy plus Input-Process-Output) was introduced by IBM.

By the mid-1980s, computer-assisted software engineering (CASE) emerged as an important force in the field of software development. Low-cost software implementing many of the popular design techniques then in use became available. Fourth generation languages redefined the role of the systems analyst for many data base-intensive applications.

Finally, we are now seeing the expansion of computer-assisted software engineering to include all aspects of software development. Current CASE tools support all areas of structured software development, with common interfaces facilitating communication between project managers, systems analysts, system implementors, and software maintenance engineers. The concepts of structured development have been expanded from looking at the structure of program loops all the way to coordinating the information flow between programmers, systems analysts, project managers, and the customer. At last, structured development promises to help *all* of the project participants.

1.5 OVERVIEW OF HIPO-II

I have managed several dozen software development projects using a wide variety of customer-specified design techniques. When given a choice, which technique did I consistently return to? The answer was HIPO. HIPO was introduced by IBM primarily as a system design tool. HIPO represents a program design as a combination of hierarchy charts (Fig. 1.5) and input-process-output (IPO) charts (Fig. 1.6) for each element in the hierarchy chart. IPO charts show input on the left, processing in the center, and outputs on the right. Most IPO charts also include arrows showing the relationship between processing steps and input/output data. HIPO is used on a large number of projects, including many extremely large software development projects performed under government contracts. Why is this technique still so popular? Some of the main reasons are as follows:

- The basic principles of HIPO, and its method of representing information, are extremely simple to teach to new programmer analysts. This is very important on projects where the staff turnover and short turnaround times for deliverables may

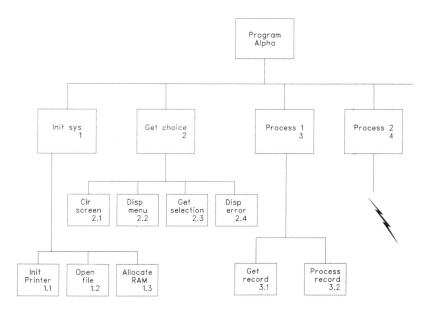

Figure 1.5   Sample HIPO Structure Chart

preclude use of any design tool that involves a lengthy learning curve.

• The outputs of HIPO are intuitively obvious to end users, even with little or no introduction to the methodology. Customers, including senior management, are not intimidated by HIPO.

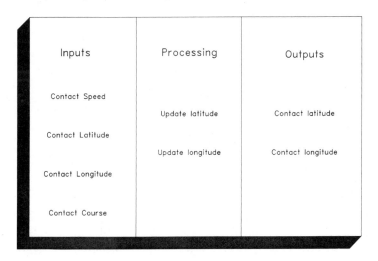

Figure 1.6   Sample IPO Chart

- HIPO enforces a hierarchical approach to modularization, leading to better designs.
- HIPO encourages a black box oriented view of program modules, focusing the designer on the input/output flows for each module. This often results in improved program maintainability and in reusable software modules.
- HIPO lends itself quite well to stepwise refinement of a problem. Designers using HIPO typically design the top one or two levels of the hierarchy, review the design with the customer, add another level of detail to the hierarchy, review the additions with the customer, etc.

Despite its advantages, HIPO slowly fell out of favor with many designers because of some serious limitations of the basic technique, including the following:

- HIPO makes no attempt to represent control flow information. Looking back to Fig. 1.5, there is no way for the reviewer or programmer to tell if modules are in a loop, are executed conditionally, etc.
- HIPO makes no provisions for global data structures or data bases.
- HIPO does not attempt to differentiate between types of functional modules on the hierarchy chart. For example, many designers become confused attempting to represent common and library modules on the hierarchy chart. Do they appear at each location called? Do they appear only once? Are they ignored?
- HIPO makes no provision for user oriented design. Menu hierarchies are not directly modeled. Sample screens and reports are not normally included in the design documentation. Prototyping is not directly supported.
- HIPO charts are difficult to produce and maintain.

HIPO-II is a modernized version of the original HIPO, retaining its strengths and eliminating its weaknesses. HIPO-II was developed by the author for use on medium-sized military software development projects. Specific changes to the original HIPO technique are shown in Fig. 1.7 and include the following:

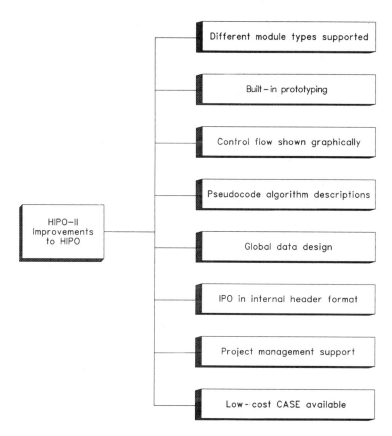

Figure 1.7   Changes to Original HIPO

1. HIPO's single class of hierarchical modules (functional process) has been expanded to include modules that represent user interaction via menus, interrupt-based modules, keyboard-activated modules, modules that are common within a design, and library modules. This improvement is addressed in detail in Chapter 2.

2. HIPO-II includes built-in, automatic prototyping capabilities. This improvement is addressed in detail in Chapter 3.

3. HIPO-II shows program control flow—including sequence, alternation, iteration, concurrency, and recursion—directly on the hierarchy chart. This improvement is addressed in detail in Chapter 4.

4. IPO processing descriptions are entered using pseudocode. The pseudocode (structured english) is also output for use by the programming team. This improvement is also addressed in Chapter 4.

5. HIPO-II includes facilities for the design and use of a common systemwide data base and global data structures. This improvement is addressed in Chapter 5.

6. The input-output portion of the IPO charts has been reformatted to match typical module internal header formats commonly used during the software implementation stage. This allows the design process to directly generate program module header entries for use by the programming team. This improvement is also addressed in Chapter 5.

7. HIPO-II is designed to directly support and interface with project management software. This is more fully described in Chapter 6.

8. Low-cost, computer-assisted software engineering support is available for HIPO-II. A typical program implementing HIPO-II is described in Chapter 9.

Chapter 7 describes the interface between the HIPO-II design effort and the program implementation effort. Chapter 8 presents a detailed method of evaluating HIPO-II versus several other popular design techniques. Appendix A summarizes HIPO-II notation. Appendix B describes how HIPO-II is used when developing software to military standards.

## chapter 2

FUNCTIONAL DECOMPOSITION with HIPO-II

I have found that the single most important step in the design process is functional decomposition. A well-structured functional decomposition will lead to clear data flows and algorithms, a usable work breakdown structure and schedule, and a manageable project. A poor functional decomposition will result in contorted, confusing data flows and algorithms, a meaningless work breakdown structure, and a project likely to fail. Let me give you an example.

A friend of mine was the project manager for a team of software professionals tasked to write a program consisting of approximately 200,000 lines of code. The government team, consisting exclusively of hardware engineers, had already prepared a functional decomposition of the entire system, including software. The software functional decomposition was prepared by people with no software background, and it was prepared before the software aspects of the problem were sufficiently analyzed or understood. The government contract insisted that the code exactly follow the structure of the government-provided functional decomposition. Predictably, the project was a disaster. The functional decomposition forms the basic framework of the entire design, and the framework was flawed. No amount of careful thought designing the data structures, data flows, control flow, and so on, could force this poorly conceived framework to work properly. After over a year and much effort it became clear that the software would never work and the project was scrapped.

HIPO-II is not just designed to make a good functional decomposition possible—most design techniques do that; HIPO-II is designed to encourage, perhaps even force you to develop a good, workable functional decomposition.

2.1 DIVIDE AND CONQUER

No reasonably complex software requirement can be understood, analyzed, or described as a single entity. The only reasonable approach to solving a complex problem is to divide it into less complex pieces. In the software design world, we call this process functional decomposition. Effective functional decomposition may be the single most important step an analyst must take when trying to understand a problem. There are four fundamentally different approaches to decomposing a problem into its components (see Fig. 2.1), and the method chosen will have a tremendous impact on how effective your decomposition is. These four methods are as follows:

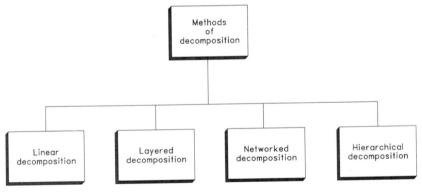

Figure 2.1   Fundamental Approaches to Decomposing a Problem

1. **Linear Decomposition:** The problem is divided into a linear list of subtasks. There is no implied order in the subtasks. More complex problems or more detailed decomposition

simply result in a larger number of subtasks. The instructions telling you how to assemble a child's toy are an example of a linear decomposition of a task (assembling the toy). Linear decomposition quickly becomes unmanageable as the size of the project increases or the required level of subtask detail increases. This approach is commonly used by early project management programs and is sometimes used by inexperienced systems analysts.

```
┌────────────────┐
│                │
│    Project     │
│    Alpha       │
│                │
└────────────────┘

     Task  1
     Task  2
     Task  3
     Task  4

        .

        .

        .

   Task  9999
```

2. *Layered Decomposition:* The entire problem is represented as layers, each showing a different aspect. Blueprints are a common example of this method. Each set of blueprints describes the entire house, but one shows electrical components, one shows framing, one shows plumbing, etc. Layering is useful if the project is not too large and the work will be performed by relatively independent groups of individuals. Large projects may combine layering with some other method of decomposition.

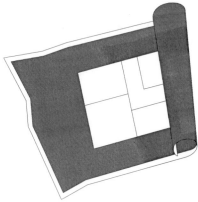

3. *Networked Decomposition:* The problem is divided into components that may represent varying levels of detail and that communicate in a free form fashion. Complex networks and data flows may result in confusing diagrams.

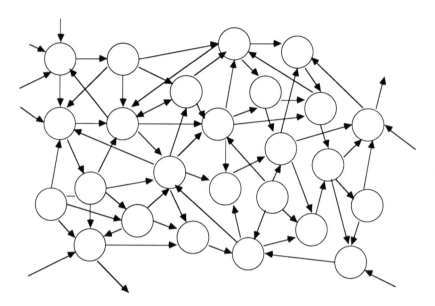

4. *Hierarchical Decomposition:* The problem is initially decomposed into a small number of tasks, normally less than eight. These tasks completely define the original problem. Each task is then further decomposed into a small number of more detailed tasks. Once again, these subtasks must completely define the portion of the problem defined by the parent task. This process is continued to whatever level of detail is required. An outline for a report is a hierarchical representation of the contents of the report.

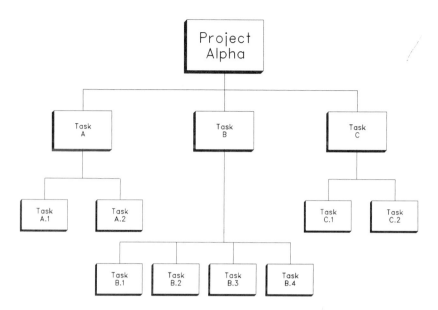

Although each of the four methods of decomposing a problem will work on small, simple projects, only hierarchical decomposition works well for large, complex projects. The use of hierarchical decomposition is especially important when the decomposition will form the basis of a software design. As shown in Fig. 2.2, hierarchical decomposition offers the following advantages:

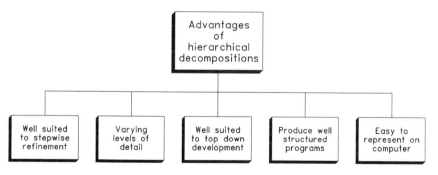

Figure 2.2   Advantages of Hierarchical Decompositions

- Hierarchical representations are well suited for stepwise refinement in which each new level of detail is fully validated against work already accomplished. A problem can be fully and accurately represented using only the first level in the hierarchy. After this level is verified with the customer, detail can be selectively added with verification against the previous level at each step.

- Hierarchical structures can be presented and reviewed at varying levels of detail. Senior management may be interested in only the top two levels. Junior programmers may be interested in only the bottom levels. Customers may wish to view the top two levels, selecting specific areas in which the detailed levels are of interest.
- Hierarchical decompositions are well suited to top-down implementation.
- Hierarchical representations tend to result in programs that are well structured, resulting in code that is easy to implement, modify, test, and maintain.
- Hierarchical structures are easy to represent and edit on a computer screen.

2.2 HIERARCHICAL REPRESENTATIONS OF DESIGNS

Surprisingly, even after deciding to decompose our problem in a hierarchical fashion, we must decide on an appropriate method of representing the hierarchy. Figure 2.3 shows a simple hierarchy represented using a traditional organizational chart type graph. Because of its intuitive clarity, this representation is commonly used in textbooks to represent hierarchical structures. This is also the method used by the original HIPO designers to represent the program hierarchy. Unfortunately, this representation is not well suited to showing large hierarchies because the charts quickly grow to an unmanageable size.

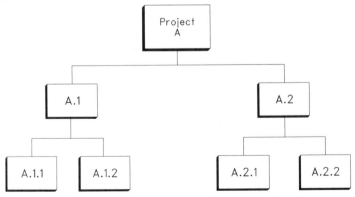

Figure 2.3 Organizational Chart Representation of a Hierarchy

Figure 2.4 shows the same hierarchy represented as nested circles. While this is popular when describing sets in mathematics classes, this representation quickly falls apart on large projects.

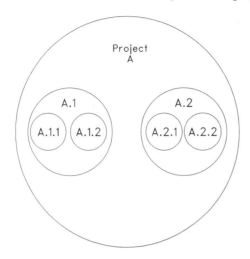

Figure 2.4   Nested Circle Representation of a Hierarchy

Warnier-Orr (a software design technique) enthusiasts would represent this hierarchy as shown in Fig. 2.5. This approach works better than the organizational chart representation, but still has difficulties on large projects as more and more levels of detail are added.

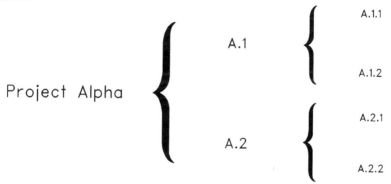

Figure 2.5   Warnier-Orr Representation of Hierarchy

Adjacency matrix and linked list representations (Fig. 2.6) are used internally by many computer algorithms and graph theory experts to represent hierarchies. They work well for large hierarchies, but are difficult for humans to interpret.

	A	A.1	A.2	A.1.1	A.1.2	A.2.1	A.2.2
A	T	T	T				
A.1	T	T		T	T		
A.2	T		T			T	T
A.1.1		T		T			
A.1.2		T			T		
A.2.1			T			T	
A.2.2			T				T

(a)

A	A	A.1	A.2				
A.1	A.1	A	A.1.1	A.1.2			
A.2	A.2	A	A.2.1	A.2.2			
A.1.1	A.1.1	A.1					
A.1.2	A.1.2	A.1					
A.2.1	A.2.1	A.2					
A.2.2	A.2.2	A.2					

(b)

Figure 2.6   Adjancy Matrix (a) and Linked List Representations (b)

Computer-aided software engineering has accelerated the trend toward representing hierarchies as shown in Fig. 2.7. Vertical hierarchy charts are easily interpreted by humans and are also easy to print on standard computer printers and terminals. Outline editors, available with many PC word processors, use vertical hierarchies.

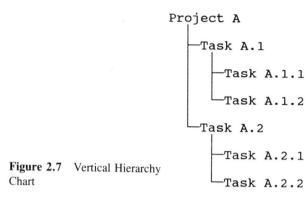

Project A

├─Task A.1

   ├─Task A.1.1

   └─Task A.1.2

└─Task A.2

   ├─Task A.2.1

   └─Task A.2.2

Figure 2.7   Vertical Hierarchy
Chart

When comparing these representations, five factors should be considered:

1. **Clarity:** How clear is the hierarchical representation to a human reader?

2. **Size:** How well does the representation work for a hierarchy consisting of many elements and many levels of decomposition?

3. **Change:** How easy is it to modify and regenerate the hierarchy as new elements are added or deleted?

4. **Printing:** Is the representation suitable for output on a standard computer printer or terminal?

5. **CASE:** Is the representation suitable for automatic computer generation by a low-cost computer and printer (e.g. PC workstation and printer)?

When deciding on the best method to incorporate into HIPO-II, each method of representing a hierarchical structure was evaluated using each of these five criteria (see Fig. 2.8). The vertical hierarchy chart is the approach used by HIPO-II.

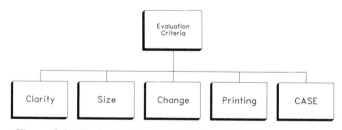

Figure 2.8   Evaluation Factors for Hierarchical Representations

2.3 MODULAR BUILDING BLOCKS

One common question inexperienced software designers ask when confronted with a large project is "Where do I start?" For most projects, the answer is "With the functional capabilities from the user's perspective." How do you do that? Suppose that we wanted to develop a new project management program called Structured Project Manager's Toolbox (SPMT).

Menu Modules

Think about the fact that a user's initial view of the program is as a collection of menu choices. Some menu choices allow data to be entered. Some menu choices allow processing to occur. Some menu choices result in reports being printed. A little thought should convince you that these menu choices define the top level functional capabilities that the user expects to see delivered. As shown in Fig. 2.9, your initial design hierarchy is simply the menu hierarchy that you propose to use in the final software. HIPO-II represents this menu hierarchy using modules which are of type *Menu*, signified by placing an (M) next to the module name on the hierarchy.

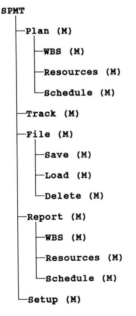

```
SPMT
  ├─Plan (M)
  │   ├─WBS (M)
  │   ├─Resources (M)
  │   └─Schedule (M)
  ├─Track (M)
  ├─File (M)
  │   ├─Save (M)
  │   ├─Load (M)
  │   └─Delete (M)
  ├─Report (M)
  │   ├─WBS (M)
  │   ├─Resources (M)
  │   └─Schedule (M)
  └─Setup (M)
```

Figure 2.9 Sample Menu Hierarchy

Keyboard Modules

Not all user-oriented functional capabilities are accessed by menu choices. Some are initiated by pressing a specially designated key on the keyboard. A function key may take the place of a menu option, a specially labeled editing key (Home, End, Page up, etc.) may cause a certain action to occur, as shown in Fig. 2.10. HIPO-II labels these keyboard-activated modules as type *Keyboard* and signifies them by placing a (K) next to the module name on the hierarchy. We will see that the key used to activate the module is defined in the module description. The key used to activate the module may also be shown on the hierarchy next to the module name.

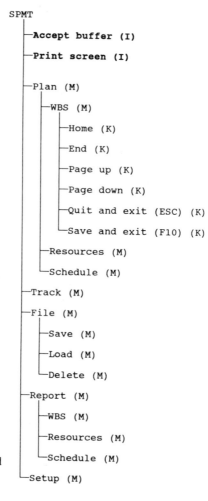

```
SPMT

   ─Accept buffer (I)

   ─Print screen (I)

   ─Plan (M)

       ─WBS (M)

           ─Home (K)

           ─End (K)

           ─Page up (K)

           ─Page down (K)

           ─Quit and exit (ESC) (K)

           ─Save and exit (F10) (K)

       ─Resources (M)

       ─Schedule (M)

   ─Track (M)

   ─File (M)

       ─Save (M)

       ─Load (M)

       ─Delete (M)

   ─Report (M)

       ─WBS (M)

       ─Resources (M)

       ─Schedule (M)

   ─Setup (M)
```

Figure 2.10 Keyboard and Interrupt Modules Sample

Interrupt Modules

One more class of user-visible functions may occur on some software projects, especially those involving communication or real time processing. An external event may interrupt the current program processing and cause temporary branching to a new program function. An example might be a periodic interrupt generated by an external or internal clock to perform some processing on a regular basis. HIPO-II calls these modules *Interrupt* modules, and labels them with an (I) next to their name. Referring once again to Fig. 2.10, we see that interrupt modules are normally shown on the top level of the hierarchy, because they may be executed from any location in the hierarchy. The event used to trigger the interrupt processing is defined in the module description, and may be shown on the hierarchy next to the module name.

On most projects, it is best to begin by functionally decomposing the problem into menu, keyboard, and interrupt modules only. These are the modules that are best understood early in the design stage, most important to the customer, and most important in providing focus to the design effort. Notice that these modules all deal with *what* the program will accomplish, not *how* the tasks will be accomplished. When the resultant functional hierarchy includes all menu, keyboard, and interrupt modules and the customer approves of that portion of the design, you are ready to begin deciding how to *accomplish* the functions already described. This detailed design refinement will be necessary under each keyboard and interrupt module, but is normally necessary only under menu modules that are nodes (have no lower level menu modules defined and actually perform some function). It should be clear that menu modules that are not nodes normally do not involve any processing; they simply result in the appropriate submenu being displayed.

Processing Modules

Internal processing necessary to implement a required functional capability is defined using modules of type *Processing* (P). Figure 2.11 is an example of a HIPO-II hierarchy showing processing modules. Once again, the appropriate letter (P) is written next to the module name on the hierarchy chart. Processing modules normally have a one-to-one correspondence with functions or subprograms when the

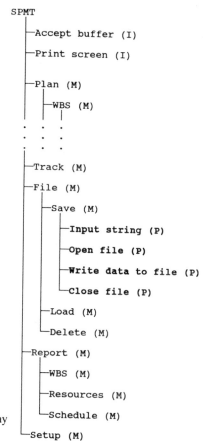

```
SPMT
    ┌─Accept buffer (I)
    ├─Print screen (I)
    ├─Plan (M)
    │   ┌─WBS (M)
    │   │   │
    .   .   .
    .   .   .
    .   .   .
    ├─Track (M)
    ├─File (M)
    │   ┌─Save (M)
    │   │   ┌─Input string (P)
    │   │   ├─Open file (P)
    │   │   ├─Write data to file (P)
    │   │   └─Close file (P)
    │   ├─Load (M)
    │   └─Delete (M)
    ├─Report (M)
    │   ┌─WBS (M)
    │   ├─Resources (M)
    │   └─Schedule (M)
    └─Setup (M)
```

Figure 2.11   Sample Hierarchy Showing Processing Modules

program is implemented. Processing modules are the only type of module supported by the original HIPO and most other design techniques.

Common Modules

One of the first problems you will run into when defining the internal processing is that many processing modules are called in multiple locations. One of the biggest advantages of structured design is that common requirements can be identified and a general purpose module written to meet the needs of several functional areas. We could show this by having lines in our hierarchy chart all go to the same module, but that gets messy fast. We could completely redefine the module each time it appeared in the hierarchy, but that would be a lot of extra work and might result in configuration control problems if changes were made to different copies of the module design. This problem may seem funny, but it has created numerous headaches for me when designing software using the original HIPO. The solution used by HIPO-II is to recognize a new module type, called *Common* (C) (see Fig. 2.12). Common modules are basically links in the design hierarchy, each of which points to a previously defined module of the same name. Changes to the single original module are reflected in the design of all related common modules.

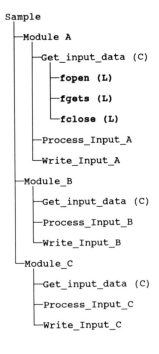

Figure 2.12   Sample Hierarchy Showing Common and Library Modules

Library Modules

Modules that are very similar to common modules are those contained in existing libraries (operating system calls also fall into this category). The problems associated with these library modules are identical to those associated with common modules, except the library modules do not point to a module already present in the design hierarchy. Note that, unlike common modules, library modules cannot be expanded to show implementation details. Referring once again to Fig. 2.12, we see that HIPO-II recognizes modules of type *Library* (L),

```
Menu   Key   Internal   Common   Library   Quit

Add a program element selected by a menu choice.
```

#	T	NAME	SCREEN	S TYPE	HEADER	P CODE
0	P	Project Alpha		N	N	N
1	M	├─Plan		N	N	N
2	M	├─Track		N	N	N
3	M	├─File		N	N	N
4	M	│ ├─Load		N	N	N
5	L	│ │ ├─fopen		N	N	N
6	L	│ │ ├─fgets		N	N	N
7	L	│ │ └─fclose		N	N	N
8	M	│ └─Save		N	N	N
9	M	└─Setup		N	N	N

Figure 2.13   Sample Computer-Generated Hierarchy Chart

in which case the module definition is not included as part of the design.

Summary of Module Types

In summary, HIPO-II supports functional decomposition into six categories of modules, with the module category shown next to each module name. Figure 2.13 shows a sample computer-generated hierarchy chart, where the module type is shown in the column labeled T. As shown in Fig. 2.14, the six recognized module categories are as follows:

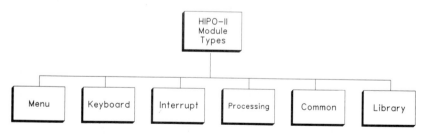

Figure 2.14   HIPO-II Module Types

1. ***Menu Modules:*** Each module represents a menu choice, with submenus represented as lower levels in the hierarchy.

2. ***Keyboard Modules:*** Each module represents a function to be performed based on a user key press.

3. *Interrupt Modules:* These modules represent processing that must occur based on some external input. Sources of interrupts typically are I/O port inputs.

4. *Processing Modules:* Each module represents logically related processing that must be accomplished by the computer program to perform some function. This is the only type of module supported by the original HIPO (and most other design techniques).

5. *Common Modules:* These are keyboard or processing modules that are used in multiple locations within the hierarchy. They are fully defined only once, normally when first identified. All other references to the module use the common definition for input, output, and processing.

6. *Library Modules:* These modules represent operating system calls or other library functions. They are shown in your design, but will not have any definitions for input, output, and processing.

2.4 PROCESS OF FUNCTIONAL DECOMPOSITION

Figure 2.15 summarizes the process of functional decomposition. You begin by working on the program menu. Each iteration of the menu design process results in a more detailed menu hierarchy. Although the customer is the biggest influencing factor during this initial process, cost and schedule considerations are certainly not ignored. In a similar fashion, the keyboard and interrupt processing is defined in an iterative fashion. The end goal is a program functional baseline consisting of menu, keyboard, and interrupt modules that,

- The customers are convinced will adequately meet their needs
- The project manager is convinced can be developed with the time, money, and other resources available
- You are convinced can be developed with reasonable risk, where risk is measured in terms of technical performance, cost, and schedule

This functional baseline often will be used as a formal or informal requirements specification that your finished design must satisfy, so be careful not to promise more than you can deliver.

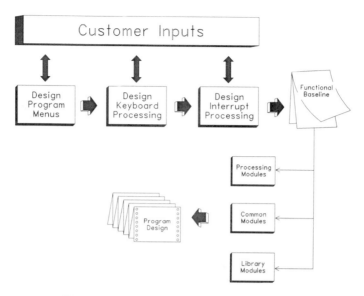

Figure 2.15   Program Functional Decomposition

Starting from the functional hierarchy, you will begin defining the internal design using processing, common, and library modules. Customer input during this stage of development normally involves answering specific technical questions that arise during the work. Cost and schedule inputs remain very important during this process to ensure that the design can be implemented with the resources available. All software designs are, to some extent, designed to cost. Technical risk considerations also play an increasing role. The following additional hints may be useful when designing internal processing:

- After you are done, start over. When you finish the second time, start over again. Good designs require several attempts.
- Look for ways to modify your decomposition to replace several related modules with one common module that is slightly more general-purpose.
- Look for ways to modify your design to use existing library modules that have already been coded and tested.
- Isolate dependencies on the operating system, file system, and design approaches to as few modules as possible.
- Emphasize clarity in the design, even at some expense in duplicate or less efficient code.

2.5 SOME EXAMPLES

Example

1. You want to represent the user interface portion of a design hierarchy. The top-level menu will contain choices for editing a document, disk operations, printing a document, and spell checking a document. The disk operations required consist of saving a document, loading a document, deleting a document, and copying a document. From the main menu, the user may press function key 1 to print the document while editing or function key 2 to spell check the document while editing. What would the resulting user interface hierarchy look like?

     Answer:

```
Word Processor
    ├─Edit Document (M)
    │    ├─Print Document (K)
    │    └─Spell Check (K)
    ├─Disk Operations (M)
    │    ├─Save Document (M)
    │    ├─Load Document (M)
    │    ├─Delete Document (M)
    │    └─Copy Document (M)
    ├─Print Document (M)
    └─Spell Check (M)
```

Example

2. In our simplified example, the tasks involved in saving a document are opening the file, writing the text to disk, and closing the file. The tasks for printing a document involve setting up the printer, printing the text, and sending a form feed to printer. Printing the text involves a loop in which each line of text is output, followed by a carriage return and line feed. Expand the hierarchy from problem 1 under the Save Document menu module and print document menu module. *Do not* expand the hierarchy under the print document keyboard module.

   Answer:

```
Word Processor
  ├─Edit Document (M)
  │   ├─Print Document (K)
  │   └─Spell Check (K)
  ├─Disk Operations (M)
  │   ├─Save Document (M)
  │   │   ├─Open File (L)
  │   │   ├─Write Text (P)
  │   │   └─Close File (L)
  │   ├─Load Document (M)
  │   ├─Delete Document (M)
  │   └─Copy Document (M)
  ├─Print Document (M)
  │   ├─Set Up Printer (P)
  │   ├─Output Text (P)
  │   │   ├─Output Line of Text (P)
  │   │   ├─Output Carriage Return (P)
  │   │   └─Output Line Feed (P)
  │   └─Send Form Feed (P)
  └─Spell Check (M)
```

Note that opening and closing a file is often a library function, although it might be a processing module if the open and close modules include some error detection checking and handling capability in your design.

Example

3. If the user presses the appropriate function key while editing the document, the program will print the current document just as if the user had selected the print option from the main menu. How will we show this in our design hierarchy?

    Answer:

```
Word Processor

 ├─Edit Document (M)

 │    ├─Print Document (K)
 │    │
 │    │    ├─Set Up Printer (C)
 │    │    │
 │    │    ├─Output Text (C)
 │    │    │
 │    │    └─Send Form Feed (C)
 │    │
 │    └─Spell Check (K)
 │
 ├─Disk Operations (M)
 │
 │    ├─Save Document (M)
 │    │
 │    │    ├─Open File (L)
 │    │    │
 │    │    ├─Write Text (P)
 │    │    │
 │    │    └─Close File (L)
 │    │
 │    ├─Load Document (M)
 │    │
 │    ├─Delete Document (M)
 │    │
 │    └─Copy Document (M)
 │
 ├─Print Document (M)
 │
 │    ├─Set Up Printer (P)
 │    │
 │    ├─Output Text (P)
 │    │
 │    │    ├─Output Line of Text (P)
 │    │    │
 │    │    ├─Output Carriage Return (P)
 │    │    │
 │    │    └─Output Line Feed (P)
 │    │
 │    └─Send Form Feed (P)
 │
 └─Spell Check (M)
```

    Notice that the copied modules are all of type common. In addition, normally it is not necessary to duplicate all of the lower levels of common modules at every location they are called. In this example, the module *output text* is shown in the new location, but the lower level modules *output line of text, output carriage return,* and *output line feed* are only shown once.

Example

4. Notice that the functions *output carriage return, output line feed,* and *send form feed* all send a single character to the printer. Notice also that this same function will be required by the routine *output line of text.* Can you improve the design?

Answer:

```
Word Processor
  ├─Edit Document (M)
  │   ├─Print Document (K)
  │   │   ├─Set Up Printer (C)
  │   │   ├─Output Text (C)
  │   │   └─Send Character to Printer (C)
  │   └─Spell Check (K)
  ├─Disk Operations (M)
  │   ├─Save Document (M)
  │   │   ├─Open File (L)
  │   │   ├─Write Text (P)
  │   │   └─Close File (L)
  │   ├─Load Document (M)
  │   ├─Delete Document (M)
  │   └─Copy Document (M)
  ├─Print Document (M)
  │   ├─Set Up Printer (P)
  │   ├─Output Text (P)
  │   │   ├─Output Line of Text (P)
  │   │   │   └─Send Character to Printer (C)
  │   │   └─Send Character to Printer (P)
  │   └─Send Character to Printer (C)
  └─Spell Check (M)
```

By combining similar functions into one module, we have significantly simplified the coding job. Writing a single module to send a character to the printer will now allow us to mark four functional hierarchy modules as complete. In addition, the general purpose nature of the routine is now clear when we decide how the module should be implemented. In general, a good design will consist primarily of common and library modules.

Although this example was very simplified, it should be clear that the basic concepts offer a structured framework for decomposing even the most complex projects down into a clear design that can be readily understood and implemented. I have personally used this type of decomposition to produce several programs, each consisting of between 35,000 and 200,000 lines of code.

chapter
3

PROTOTYPING
with
HIPO-II

As technical manager for a project to develop new tactical decision aids, I began the project by designing all menus, data entry screens, and sample reports. These were implemented as a fully functional program shell within two weeks. Our initial design walk-throughs consisted of the customers operating the program and explaining desired changes to the user interface, reports, available options, and so on, while sitting in front of the terminal. Before we began work on the detailed program design, we had a complete model of the final program. In addition to the improved customer involvement in the design process, this approach offered two unexpected benefits:

1. Each programmer was required to spend some time operating the prototype. This approach was very effective in providing an overview of the project to the programming team.
2. Throughout development, the prototype was used for all demonstrations to visiting VIPs, thus eliminating wasted time

and potential embarrassment attempting to get a partially complete program operating for a demo.

A fundamental principle of both HIPO and HIPO-II is that the success of any project is directly proportionate to the amount of customer involvement in the design process. One of the best ways to improve customer involvement in a program design effort is to demonstrate a working model of the final program early in the design stage. This prototyping is encouraged in HIPO-II through built-in support for automatic prototyping.

In general, prototyping is especially effective on projects in which the user interface to the system is a significant component of the design. This is true for most systems intended for widespread distribution and use by average users. Some highly technical, embedded, or real time systems may have very little (if any) user interface design required, in which case HIPO-II prototyping capabilities are not especially useful. Prototyping or modeling of accuracies, timing, data flows, etc., is more significant for these applications, although this is not directly supported by HIPO-II.

3.1 LEVELS OF PROTOTYPING

Figure 3.1 shows seven levels of system prototyping. These are defined as follows:

1. *Dialogue Prototypes*—the prototype simulates the interaction between the computer and the end user via simulated program menus

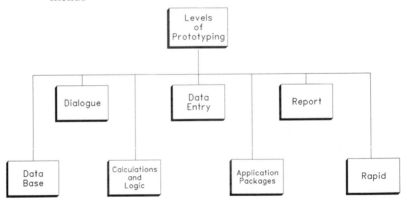

Figure 3.1   Seven Levels of Prototyping

2. *Data Entry Prototypes*—the prototype simulates data entry screens

3. *Report Prototypes*—the prototype simulates output reports using dummy data

4. *Data Base Prototypes*—the prototype includes a version of the final data base with dummy data. It is useful for demonstrating interactive query capabilities on data base intensive applications.

5. *Calculations and Logic*—the prototype simulates program calculations and logic, often including models of processing delay and math accuracy

6. *Application Package*—a general purpose application similar to the software being developed is used as the prototype

7. *Rapid Prototyping*—rapid prototyping involves the rapid development of a fully functional version of the final program, although some capabilities may be limited. User feedback is used to continuously refine this model until an acceptable version is generated.

HIPO-II prototyping tools focus on levels 1, 2, and 3, which are the areas applicable to the widest range of user applications. The HIPO-II generated prototype models all program menus, data entry screens, report screens, and overlays. Program options selected using special purpose keys (special function keys, page up, page down, etc.) can be demonstrated, as well as interrupt processing. In summary, we will see that HIPO-II allows powerful modeling and demonstration of the program's complete program user interface prior to commencing detailed internal design. This is accomplished in HIPO-II by describing specific screen formats for menu, keyboard, and interrupt modules.

3.2 HIPO-II PROTOTYPING SCREEN FORMAT

Figure 3.2 shows the top-level menu choices available with a representative computer-assisted software engineering (CASE) tool which implements HIPO-II (Structured Designer's Tool Box™). Selecting *Design* allows the systems analyst to design the program's data structures and functional hierarchy. Selecting *Test* activates the automatic prototyping capabilities and displays the screen shown in Fig.

```
Design  Test  File  Report  Setup  Quit
Design a Program
```

Figure 3.2   HIPO-II CASE Top-Level Menu Choices

3.3. Each area of the prototyping screen will be described individually in the paragraphs that follow. A complete description of the CASE tool being used to illustrate these concepts can be found in Chapter 9.

Menu Lines

This area of the screen displays a command line menu in a format similar to that used by LOTUS 1-2-3™. The user selects menu choices either by pressing the first letter of the choice or by moving the menu cursor to the desired selection and pressing return. Although the final program may implement the menu as pull down windows, pop up windows, etc., this simple interface is adequate to demonstrate and validate the selected menu choices.

Prompt Area

This area of the screen displays a one-line menu prompt that changes as the user moves the menu highlight to different choices.

```
Menu choices line 1.
Menu choices line 2.
Menu specific prompt line.



         Output Screens
                    Reports
                    Overlays
```

Figure 3.3   HIPO-II CASE Prototype Screen Layout

Display Area

The remainder of the screen is used to display sample screens, overlays, and reports. Sample screens and reports use the entire display area. Sample overlays are windows that are overlaid on top of the previously displayed screen. Sample outputs are generated by the designer and associated with specific menu, keyboard, or interrupt modules. Figure 3.4 shows a sample user interface design hierarchy in which sample outputs are defined. Modules with an associated sample output have a sample output number shown next to the module name.

```
Project Alpha

  ┌─Design (M)

  │   ┌─Data (M)     [1-Screen]

  │   └─Program (M) [2-Screen]

  │       ┌─Add_Task (M) [3-Overlay]

  │       └─Delete_Task (M) [4-Overlay]

  ├─Test (M)

  ├─Report (M)

  │   ┌─Report_1 (M) [5-Report]

  │   └─Report_2 (M) [6-Report]

  ├─File (M)

  └─Setup (M)
```

Figure 3.4 Sample Outputs Associated with Menu, Keyboard, and Interrupt Modules

Sample outputs may contain any character from the IBM character set, including extended characters. This allows the designer to include line drawing characters, block characters, etc. Screen attributes are modifiable by the designer to show colors, reverse video, blinking, etc. Figures 3.5, 3.6, and 3.7 show a sample screen, overlay, and report generated using these characters. In addition, sample outputs can be copied, modified, deleted, written to disk, and read from disk if desired.

```
Add   Modify   Specify   Header   Process   Delete   Range   View   Goto   Quit

Add new program element.
```

#	T	NAME	SCREEN	S TYPE	HEADER	P
0	P	Project Alpha		N	N	N
1	M	├─Design		N	N	N
2	M	├─Data		N	N	N
3	M	└─Program		N	N	N
4	M	├─Test		N	N	N
5	M	├─File		N	N	N
6	M	├─Report		N	N	N
7	M	├─Report 1		N	N	N
8	M	└─Report 2		N	N	N
9	M	└─Setup		N	N	N

```
Maximum tasks: 1500                                                    V
```

Figure 3.5   Sample Screen

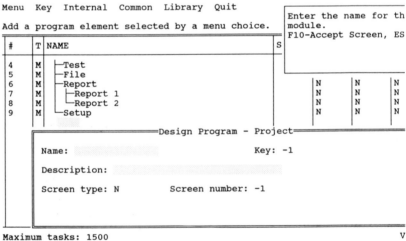

```
Menu   Key   Internal   Common   Library   Quit
                                                    Enter the name for th
Add a program element selected by a menu choice.   module.
                                                    F10-Accept Screen, ES
```

#	T	NAME	S
4	M	├─Test	
5	M	├─File	
6	M	├─Report	
7	M	├─Report 1	
8	M	└─Report 2	
9	M	└─Setup	

```
                          ═Design Program - Project═

   Name:                           Key: -1

   Description:

   Screen type: N         Screen number: -1
```

```
Maximum tasks: 1500                                                    V
```

Figure 3.6   Sample Overlay

William H. Roetzheim & Assoc.
3891 American Avenue
La Mesa, CA 92041
(619) 464-0182

#	T	NAME	SCREEN	S TYPE	HEADER	P
0	P	Project Alpha		N	N	N
1	M	─Design		N	N	N
2	M	├─Data		N	N	N
3	M	└─Program		N	N	N
4	M	─Test		N	N	N
5	M	─File		N	N	N
6	M	─Report		N	N	N
7	M	├─Report 1		N	N	N
8	M	└─Report 2		N	N	N
9	M	└─Setup		N	N	N

***** Any Key to Continue. *****

Figure 3.7   Sample Report

3.3 MODELING PROGRAM MENUS

Recall that the HIPO-II functional hierarchy consists of six classes of modules:

1. Menu   4. Processing
2. Key   5. Common
3. Interrupt   6. Library

As you add menu modules to your design hierarchy, HIPO-II-based tools can automatically use this information to generate a sample command line menu interface. Figure 3.8 shows a sample design hierarchy, and Fig. 3.9 shows the command line menu that would be displayed initially. If the user selects the *File* option from the command line menu, Structured Designer's Toolbox (SDT) would then display the command line menu shown in Fig. 3.10. As the user moves the menu cursor, SDT automatically displays a description of the menu choice on the prompt line of the screen. These description lines are entered by the designer in the description field as part of the module definition screen (see Fig. 3.11). The module data entry form also allows the designer to designate a sample output to be associated with this menu option. Recall that sample outputs can be of type Screen (S), Overlay (O), or Report (R). Typically, these outputs would be assigned as follows:

```
Project Alpha
    ├─Design (M)
    ├─Test (M)
    ├─Report (M)
    ├─File (M)
    │     ├─Save (M)
    │     ├─Retrieve (M)
    │     ├─Delete (M)
    │     └─Convert (M)
    └─Setup (M)
```

Figure 3.8 Sample Design Hierarchy

```
┌────────────────────────────────────────────────────────┐
│ Design  Test  Report  File  Setup  Quit                │
│                                                         │
│ Operations to/from disk.                                │
│ ═══════════════════════════════════════════════════════│
│                                                         │
│                                                         │
│                                                         │
│                                                         │
└────────────────────────────────────────────────────────┘
```

Figure 3.9 Generated Command Line Menu

```
┌────────────────────────────────────────────────────────┐
│ Save  Retrieve  Delete  Convert  Quit                  │
│                                                         │
│ Save project file to disk.                              │
│ ═══════════════════════════════════════════════════════│
│                                                         │
│                                                         │
│                                                         │
│                                                         │
└────────────────────────────────────────────────────────┘
```

Figure 3.10 Command Line Menu After Selecting FILE

```
┌═══════════════Design Program - Project═══════════════┐
│                                                        │
│ Name: Save                       Key: -1               │
│ Description: Operations to/from disk.                  │
│ Screen type: N         Screen number: -1               │
│                                                        │
└────────────────────────────────────────────────────────┘
```

Figure 3.11 Command Line Menu Prompts are Entered When Defining a Module

1. Menu modules that have submenus defined normally will not
include any sample outputs (Fig. 3.12).

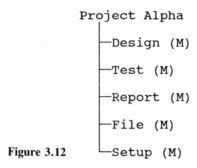

Project Alpha

─Design (M)

─Test (M)

─Report (M)

─File (M)

Figure 3.12   ─Setup (M)

2. Menu modules that display full screen tables, matrices, etc.,
will include a sample output of type Screen (S) (Fig. 3.13).

```
Project Alpha

 ─Data Maintenance (M)
   └─Enter PIM (M) [1-Screen]
 ─Report (M)
 ─File (M)
 ─Setup (M)
```

PIM #	COURSE	SPEED	DURATION
01	▓▓▓▓▓	▓▓▓	▓▓▓▓▓▓

Figure 3.13

3. Menu modules that overlay a data entry window on the current screen will include a sample output of type Overlay (O) (Fig. 3.14).

```
Project Alpha
  ├─Data Maintenance (M)
  ├─Report (M)
  ├─File (M)
  └─Setup (M)
       └─Enter Own Ship (M)  [1-Overlay]
```

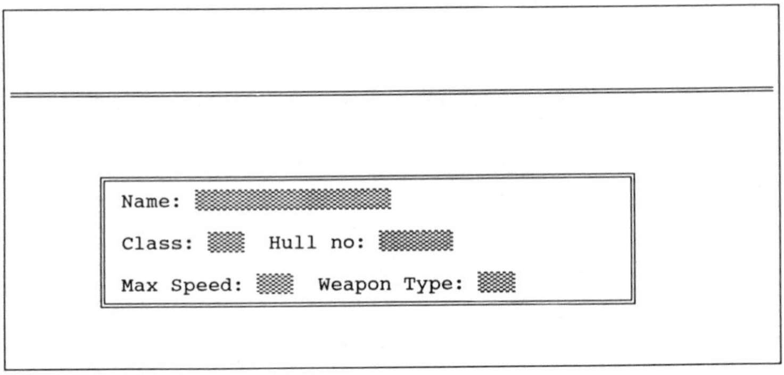

Figure 3.14

4. Menu modules that activate an internal function will normally include a sample output of type Overlay (O) which displays a prompt informing the user of the processing that is being performed (Fig. 3.15).

```
Project Alpha
  ├─Data Maintenance (M)
  │   └─Sort Data Base (M) [1-Overlay]
  ├─Report (M)
  ├─File (M)
  └─Setup (M)
```

```
┌──────────────────────────────────────────────────────────────┐
│                                                              │
│                                                              │
│  ══════════════════════════════════════════════════════════ │
│                                                              │
│                                                              │
│         ┌─────────────────────────────┐                     │
│         │ Sorting Data Base.          │                     │
│         └─────────────────────────────┘                     │
│                                                              │
│                                                              │
│                                                              │
│                                                              │
└──────────────────────────────────────────────────────────────┘
```

Figure 3.15

5. Menu modules that print a report will include a sample output of type Report (R). HIPO-II prints reports to the screen. Reports can be simplified, but normally should include column headings and a sample layout (Fig. 3.16).

```
Project Alpha
  ├─Data Maintenance (M)
  ├─Report (M)
  │   └─PIM (M) [1-Report]
  ├─File (M)
  └─Setup (M)
```

```
┌──────────────────────────────────────────────────────────────┐
│                                                              │
│                                                              │
│  ══════════════════════════════════════════════════════════ │
│  PIM #   COURSE   SPEED   DURATION   LAT       LONG          │
│   01      180      10       30       32.33N    163.29W       │
│   02      173      11       45       32.10N    163.29W       │
│  etc.    etc.     etc.     etc.      etc.      etc.          │
│                                                              │
│                                                              │
│                                                              │
│                                                              │
└──────────────────────────────────────────────────────────────┘
```

Figure 3.16

While running the prototype, if the user selects a menu module that is a node (has no children) for which you have not defined a sample output, SDT will automatically display a prompt confirming the selection (Fig. 3.17).

```
Project Alpha
   ├─Data Maintenance (M)
   ├─Report (M)
   ├─File (M)
   │   └─Delete_File (M)
   └─Setup (M)
```

```
┌─────────────────────────────────────────────────────┐
│                                                       │
│                                                       │
│ ═══════════════════════════════════════════════════ │
│                                                       │
│                                                       │
│          ┌─────────────────────────────┐             │
│          │ Executing Delete_File       ║             │
│          └─────────────────────────────┘             │
│                                                       │
│                                                       │
│                                                       │
└─────────────────────────────────────────────────────┘
```

Figure 3.17

3.4 MODELING KEY-ACTIVATED PROCESSING

Most programs involve some special processing when the user presses a special function key or a labeled keyboard key (PgUp, Home, End, Up Arrow, etc.). Normally, the specific function activated is based on the user's location in the functional hierarchy when the key is pressed.

At each level in the menu hierarchy, Structured Designer's Toolbox (SDT) determines what key modules are defined (see Fig. 3.18). If the user presses a special-purpose key, SDT determines if the key is one of those defined. Looking at Fig. 3.19, if the user pressed the Home key, SDT would display Overlay 3.

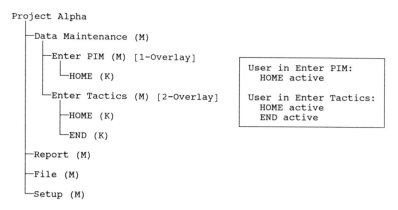

```
Project Alpha

  ─Data Maintenance (M)

      ─Enter PIM (M) [1-Overlay]
                                          ┌─────────────────────────────┐
          └─HOME (K)                      │ User in Enter PIM:          │
                                          │    HOME active              │
      └─Enter Tactics (M) [2-Overlay]     │                             │
                                          │ User in Enter Tactics:      │
          ─HOME (K)                       │    HOME active              │
                                          │    END active               │
          └─END (K)                       └─────────────────────────────┘

  ─Report (M)

  ─File (M)

  └─Setup (M)
```

Figure 3.18

```
Project Alpha

  ─Data Maintenance (M)

      ─Enter PIM (M) [1-Overlay]
                                          ┌─────────────────────────────┐
          └─HOME (K) [3-Overlay]          │ User in Enter PIM           │
                                          └─────────────────────────────┘
      └─Enter Tactics (M) [2-Overlay]

          ─HOME (K) [4-Overlay]

          └─END (K) [5-Overlay]

  ─Report (M)

  ─File (M)

  └─Setup (M)
```

Figure 3.19

This capability can be used to model quite detailed screen operations. For example, suppose we want to model a cursor moving around a data entry screen. We begin with the hierarchy shown in Fig. 3.20. When the user selects the ENTER DATA menu option, Overlay 1 is displayed (Fig. 3.21). The design hierarchy tells us that from this location, the following special-purpose keys are available:

1. Home
2. Up arrow
3. Down arrow
4. Forward arrow
5. Back arrow
6. End

```
Project Alpha
  ├─Data Maintenance (M)
  │    ├─Enter Data (M) [1-Overlay]
  │    │    ├─HOME (K) [2-Overlay]
  │    │    ├─UP ARROW (K) [3-Overlay]
  │    │    ├─DOWN ARROW (K) [4-Overlay]
  │    │    ├─FORWARD ARROW (K) [5-Overlay]
  │    │    ├─BACK ARROW (K) [6-Overlay]
  │    │    └─END (K) [7-Overlay]
  │    └─Enter Tactics (M)
  ├─Report (M)
  ├─File (M)
  └─Setup (M)
```

```
┌─────────────────────────┐
│   User in Enter data     │
└─────────────────────────┘
```

Figure 3.20

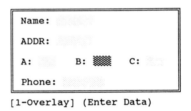

[1-Overlay] (Enter Data)

Figure 3.21   Overlay 1

We tell SDT that each of these six modules has an overlay associated with it, numbered Overlay 2 through Overlay 7. We begin by copying the sample output from Overlay 1 to each of these six new overlays. Now, for each of these overlays we modify the overlay to show the new location for the cursor after the user presses the appropriate key (Fig. 3.22). When running the demo, the user can now see a visual representation of how the various special-purpose keys move the cursor around the data entry screen.

For most applications, it is not necessary or desirable to define a sample output for **every** possible action. Select areas of the design where confusion is possible and define a sample output for those specific areas. For example, you might want to define all keyboard keys for a single data entry screen to demonstrate the concept. For all

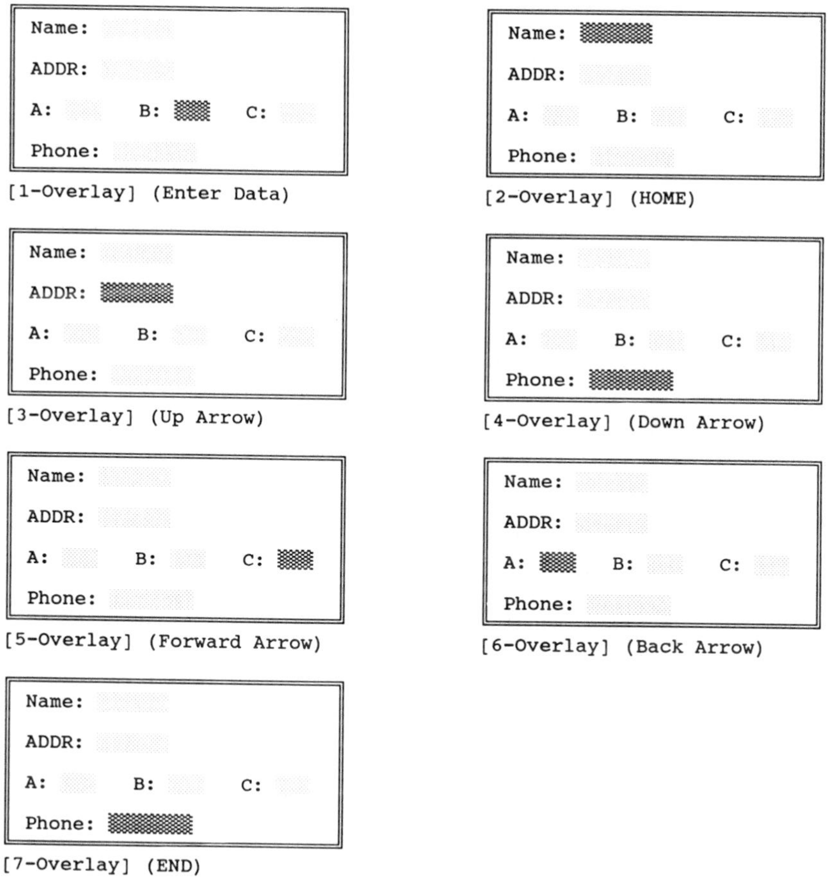

```
Name: ▓▓▓▓
ADDR: ▓▓▓▓
A: ▓▓   B: ▓▓▓   C: ▓▓▓
Phone: ▓▓▓▓▓
```
[1-Overlay] (Enter Data)

```
Name: ▓▓▓▓▓▓
ADDR: ▓▓▓▓
A: ▓▓   B: ▓▓   C: ▓▓
Phone: ▓▓▓▓▓
```
[2-Overlay] (HOME)

```
Name: ▓▓▓▓
ADDR: ▓▓▓▓▓▓▓
A: ▓▓   B: ▓▓   C: ▓▓
Phone: ▓▓▓▓▓
```
[3-Overlay] (Up Arrow)

```
Name: ▓▓▓▓
ADDR: ▓▓▓▓
A: ▓▓   B: ▓▓   C: ▓▓
Phone: ▓▓▓▓▓▓
```
[4-Overlay] (Down Arrow)

```
Name: ▓▓▓▓
ADDR: ▓▓▓▓
A: ▓▓   B: ▓▓   C: ▓▓▓
Phone: ▓▓▓▓▓
```
[5-Overlay] (Forward Arrow)

```
Name: ▓▓▓▓
ADDR: ▓▓▓▓
A: ▓▓▓   B: ▓▓   C: ▓▓
Phone: ▓▓▓▓▓
```
[6-Overlay] (Back Arrow)

```
Name: ▓▓▓▓
ADDR: ▓▓▓▓
A: ▓▓   B: ▓▓   C: ▓▓
Phone: ▓▓▓▓▓▓▓
```
[7-Overlay] (END)

Figure 3.22

other data entry screens, you might just define the basic screen to show the overall layout.

When used properly, this capability is extremely powerful in demonstrating program functioning. It is especially useful when demonstrating functioning performed by pressing special function keys, where the action taken may be quite significant (split the screen into two windows, etc.).

While running the prototype, if the user selects a special purpose key for which a keyboard module is defined but for which no output is specified, SDT automatically displays a prompt confirming the selection.

3.5 MODELING INTERRUPT PROCESSING

At each menu level Structured Designer's Toolbox (SDT) remembers what interrupt modules are included in the functional hierarchy. External interrupt processing is modeling by mapping the interrupt to a keyboard key for the prototype. For example, the designer may designate that an interrupt on the serial port is simulated by pressing Function Key 1 on the keyboard. Interrupt module definitions include a field telling SDT which keyboard key activates the module. Associated with each interrupt module would be an overlay displaying a window containing a prompt message explaining which interrupt occurred.

During the design demonstration, the user may be in the middle of reviewing an editing screen (Fig. 3.23). An interrupt is simulated by pressing the appropriate keyboard key and SDT displays a prompt (Fig. 3.24). The user presses any key to return to the original position in the program hierarchy.

While running the prototype, if the user selects a special-purpose key for which an interrupt module is defined but for which no output is specified, SDT automatically displays a prompt confirming the selection.

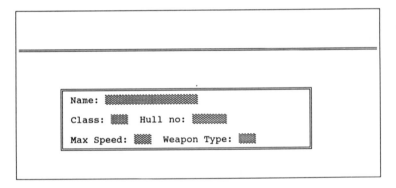

Figure 3.23   User in Edit Screen

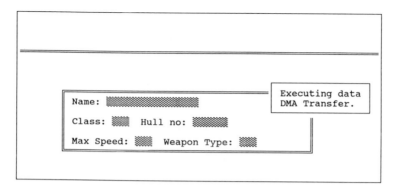

Figure 3.24

3.6 USING HIPO-II PROTOTYPING CAPABILITIES

It is important to remember that HIPO-II prototyping capabilities should be used only as much as necessary to clarify the design. The first step normally is to define the program's menu hierarchy. The prototyping capabilities of HIPO-II can then be used to demonstrate the menu in operation, with printed versions of the actual hierarchy used to provide an overview. Remember that this prototyping capability involves no extra work on the part of the designer.

After the customer approves the initial menu hierarchy, it usually is best to define sample reports for the appropriate menu choices. Do not be afraid to include textual descriptions of report features along with the sample format, if appropriate (see Fig. 3.25). These should be

```
PIM #    COURSE    SPEED    DURATION    LAT        LONG
  01      180       10        30        32.33N     163.29W
  02      173       11        45        32.10N     163.29W
 etc.     etc.     etc.      etc.       etc.       etc.

       NOTE:   lats and longs will be calculated.
               Errors will be flagged with asterisks.
```

Figure 3.25

reviewed with the customer. When the reports are approved, it normally is wise to define a sample data entry screen for every data entry screen to be included in the final program. Do not worry about things like moving the cursor around, but be specific about field prompts, field layouts on the screen, etc. These should be reviewed with the customer.

When the data entry screens are approved, expand any area of the user interface that is not clear with supporting sample screens and outputs. As appropriate, review these with the customer. Figure 3.26 summarizes this process.

After the user interface is firmed up and the prototype is completely approved, this becomes the foundation for all later design work (processing modules). The user will expect the final program to look like the prototype (in terms of functionality), but usually will not be overly concerned about changes in the internal processing during development (as long as the answers displayed are correct!). The design prototype can be used to orient new programmers into the goals of the project. In addition, it is sometimes desirable to begin work on the User's Manual prior to completion of the final program. The prototype allows the User's Manual to be written (complete with sample screens) at an early stage in the project.

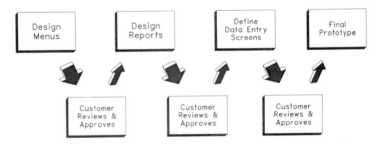

Figure 3.26   Using HIPO-II Prototyping Capabilities

chapter 4

ALGORITHM DESIGN with HIPO-II

The heart of many scientific, engineering, and military software applications is the specific algorithms used in the program. This algorithmic definition includes both control flow design for module calls and detailed logic for processing modules. Figure 4.1 shows a portion of a simplified program design. Are the modules *Update Polynomial* and *Analyze Error* called once or multiple times in a loop? What exactly is involved in these modules? If you were a programmer, could you write the program from this information? Of course not. Clearly, we need a method of documenting program control flow logic and algorithms.

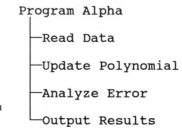

Figure 4.1 Simplified Program Design

The original HIPO technique documented program algorithms in the process portion of input-process-output charts. Figure 4.2 shows a sample HIPO-II algorithm description. No control flow information was shown on the hierarchy chart, and processing descriptions normally did not include any detailed descriptions of control flow. The failure of HIPO to adequately represent program control flow on the hierarchy charts is considered by many to be one of its primary flaws.

HIPO-II modifies this approach slightly by adding control flow information to the hierarchy chart and using a more formal pseudocode for the processing block of input-process-output charts. This chapter describes these two changes in more detail.

Inputs	Processing	Outputs
Contact Speed		
	Update latitude	Contact latitude
Contact Latitude		
	Update longitude	Contact longitude
Contact Longitude		
Contact Course		

Figure 4.2   Sample HIPO Algorithm Description

4.1 GRAPHICAL CONTROL FLOW REPRESENTATION

Many analysts require a design technique that will represent control flow information directly on the hierarchy charts. They believe that a graphical representation of this information is critical to their ability to quickly communicate an overview of the program's function. HIPO-II modifies the basic hierarchy chart format slightly to allow each of the five basic control flow constructs to be represented graphically. These will be illustrated individually in the paragraphs that follow:

Sequence.   By default, modules defined in the HIPO-II hierarchy are assumed to be processed sequentially from top to bottom. A single line is used to connect each module to the hierarchy.

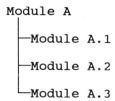

```
Module A

    ├─Module A.1

    ├─Module A.2

    └─Module A.3
```

Iteration.   Progam looping is represented using double lines to connect each module to the hierarchy. HIPO-II does not attempt to differentiate between FOR . . . NEXT, WHILE . . . WEND, and DO . . . UNTIL type loops (Fig. 4.3) on the hierarchy chart, although this information is documented in the processing description for the module.

```
Module B

    ╠═Module A.1

    ╠═Module A.2

    ╚═Module A.3
```

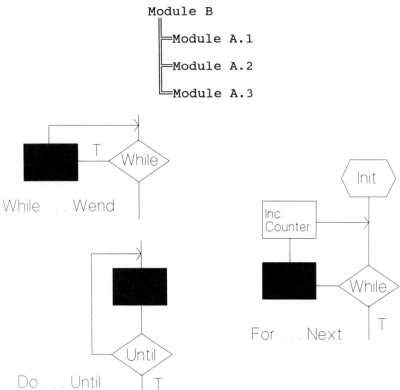

Figure 4.3

Alternation.   Alternation is represented using a brace to connect the affected modules to the hierarchy. HIPO-II does not attempt to differentiate between IF...THEN and CASE type constructs on the hierarchy chart. Once again, this level of detail is shown in the processing description for the module.

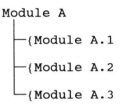

```
Module A

   ─{Module A.1

   ─{Module A.2

   ─{Module A.3
```

Concurrency.   HIPO-II supports design of concurrent programs. Concurrent modules are connected to the hierarchy using an epsilon character. If you are familiar with concurrent processing, you might notice that the HIPO-II concurrency construct works similar to COBEGIN and COEND, with critical sections of code (if any) defined in the module processing description.

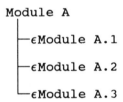

```
Module A

   ─εModule A.1

   ─εModule A.2

   ─εModule A.3
```

Recursion.   Recursion in HIPO-II programs is documented by showing one module in the hierarchy calling itself. The lower level module will be specified as type *Common* using HIPO-II's module categories. The recursion conditions are defined in the module processing description.

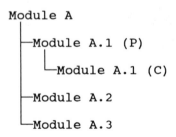

```
Module A

   ─Module A.1 (P)

       ─Module A.1 (C)

   ─Module A.2

   ─Module A.3
```

Of course, control flow constructs can be nested. Figure 4.4 shows part of a program design that contains a loop with an embedded IF . . . THEN test.

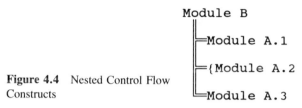

Figure 4.4   Nested Control Flow
Constructs

HIPO-II graphical control flow constructs have been selected to have the following properties:

- They are easy to recognize and understand with very little explanation. End users are comfortable with the representations.
- They are easy to produce using a low-cost computer and printer with line-drawing capability. Computer terminals with line-drawing character sets in ROM do not need graphics capability.
- They are easy to draw and change by hand when a computer is not available.

Although the HIPO-II graphical representations of control flow information are good for quick overviews of the program logic, obviously they are not sufficiently detailed to allow a programmer to produce code directly from the hierarchy chart. This detailed representation of program logic will be addressed in the following section.

4.2 DETAILED ALGORITHM DEFINITION

We need a method of representing the detailed program logic in sufficient detail to allow a programmer to properly implement our design. One approach used by many design techniques (for example, Warnier-Orr and Action Diagrams) is to expand the hierarchy chart down to the level of individual lines of code, including details of conditional logic (Fig. 4.5 shows a fragment of a Warnier-Orr which is detailed enough to code from.). Although this approach allows automatic generation of code and detailed checking of program logic, it has at least one significant disadvantage. Producing and maintaining

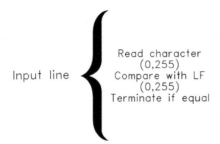

Input line

Read character
(0,255)
Compare with LF
(0,255)
Terminate if equal

Figure 4.5   Warnier-Orr Decomposes
to Individual Statements

the design can easily become prohibitively expensive. In effect, an extremely expensive, top-level designer is forced to perform detailed design work that would be better performed by a junior programmer. The designer should specify the overall program control flow and algorithms, but implementation details should be left to the programming team.

HIPO-II uses pseudocode, also called structured english, to represent detailed module algorithms. Pseudocode was chosen because it is the most compact and efficient method of representing general designs that is available today. Pseudocode is a description of the program logic with the following characteristics (summarized in Fig. 4.6):

- The wording is extremely concise

```
If the track speed is less than 25 Knots, call the routine to
update the Kalman filter variables.

                      becomes

if (track.speed < 25) update Kalman filter
```

- Block structuring is shown using braces (or BEGIN and END keywords) and indentation

```
While (track.number < 50)
Read updated data
If (track.type is hostile)
Update threat warning file
Notify operator of threat


                          becomes

While (track.number < 50) {
      Read updated data;
      If (track.type is hostile) {
            Update threat warning file;
            Notify operator of threat;
      }
}
```

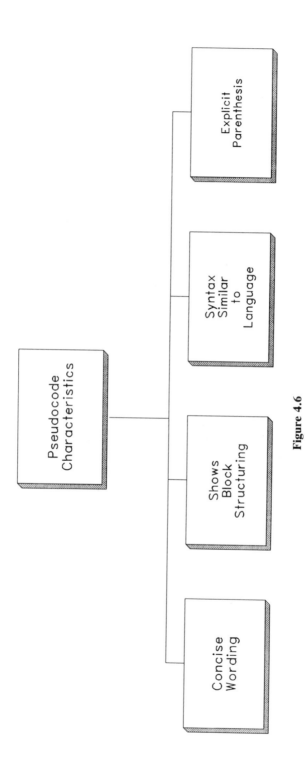

Figure 4.6

- Algorithm logic uses syntax similar to the language which will be used to implement the actual program

- Explicit parenthesis are used to avoid all expression ambiguities

```
A = B * C + 3 * 4 / 6;

                        becomes

A = (B * C) + ((3 * 4) / 6);
```

All module input and output variables should be shown in capital letters. Local (internal) variables should be lower case. This permits computer-assisted software engineering to automatically perform the following checks:

1. Ensure that input and output variables that were defined in the module header (input and output portion of IPO charts) are referenced in the processing description.
2. Ensure that all input and output variables defined in the module processing description are defined in the module header.

The freeform nature of HIPO-II's algorithm representation allows other information to be included, when appropriate. For example, some internal logic can best be represented using a truth table. The truth table would be embedded in the structured english description of the module. If the algorithm is to be taken from an existing book or magazine, the appropriate reference can be directly included. Unusual timing, accuracy, or storage allocation requirements also can be included in this area.

4.3 SUMMARY

HIPO-II uses freeform pseudocode to represent detailed program logic. Pseudocode includes only the level of detail appropriate for the problem being described. For some modules, this will be a single descriptive line. For other modules, this might include detailed pseudocode, truth tables, timing accuracy and storage allocation requirements, and references. In keeping to the overall HIPO-II design philosophy, the algorithm design is only as complex as the problem requires.

```
┌──────────┐
│ chapter  │
│    5     │
└──────────┘
```

DATA DESIGN
with
HIPO-II

In earlier chapters, we discussed how HIPO-II can be used to design a program's user interface (user-oriented design) and a program's control flow and algorithms (algorithm-oriented design). The third vital component of effective software design is structuring of the data base and definition of data flows (data-oriented design). For many applications, especially those that are business related, the data-oriented design may be the single most important aspect of your final design document. In this chapter, we will describe how HIPO-II allows you to easily design and maintain both a program's global data structures and its data flows.

5.1 DATA STRUCTURE DESIGN WITH HIPO-II

The original HIPO made no provisions for a global data base containing information available to all program modules. This deficiency hindered efforts by analysts to define data base structures, a crucial area for many applications. HIPO-II corrects this problem by including provisions for designing global data structures, using a hierarchical format similar to that used during functional decomposition. These data definitions normally include all data elements that are available to program functions and that are not explicitly passed to individual modules (that is, all external or global data). External data might include data files or data available from a data base management system. Global data consists of variables and data structures that are accessible from all program elements.

HIPO-II represents the external data structures hierarchically using a format similar to that used to represent the program's functional hierarchy (Fig. 5.1).

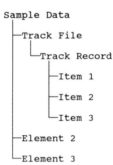

```
Sample Data

 ├─Track File

 │   └─Track Record

 │        ├─Item 1

 │        ├─Item 2

 │        └─Item 3

 ├─Element 2

 └─Element 3
```

Figure 5.1 External Data Structures are Represented Hierarchically

Data types are written in parentheses next to each data element (Fig. 5.2). Although the data types used will vary based on your development environment, some typical types are File (DF), Record (R), Structure (S), Bit (B), Character (C), Unsigned Character (UC), Integer (I), Unsigned Integer (UI), Long Integer (L), Unsigned Long Integer (UL), Floating point number (F), and Double precision floating point number (D). Data elements of type file, record, and structure represent aggregates of data. Other data types in this example represent physical units of data in the target language.

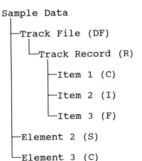

```
Sample Data

 ├─Track File (DF)

 │   └─Track Record (R)

 │        ├─Item 1 (C)

 │        ├─Item 2 (I)

 │        └─Item 3 (F)

 ├─Element 2 (S)

 └─Element 3 (C)
```

Figure 5.2 Data Types are Shown in Parenthesis

If the data element is actually an array of the appropriate type, the size of the array is shown next to the data element (Fig. 5.3). In this example, strings are represented as arrays of characters.

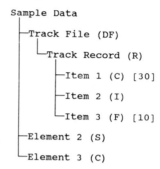

Figure 5.3   Array Sizes are Shown in Braces

For data elements representing aggregates of data (data file, record within a data file, or data structure), the estimated quantity of aggregate elements is shown next to the data element (Fig. 5.4). Structures are a composite data type. The data type determines whether the number represents an array size or aggregate quantity consisting of one or more data elements.

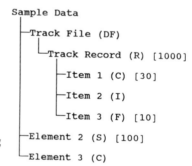

Figure 5.4   Example Showing Aggregates of Data

Matrices are represented by showing both matrix dimensions separated by a comma (Fig. 5.5).

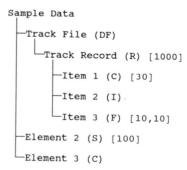

Figure 5.5   Example Showing Matrices

Figure 5.6 shows a sample CASE data entry form for a HIPO-II data element (this form is used by *Structured Designer's Toolbox*™). When entering data elements, the fields have the following meanings:

1. *Name*—the name of the data element. As you define module data flows, the data elements used are validated automatically against this name.
2. *Type*—the type of data represented by this element (file, record, integer, etc.)
3. *Size*—if the data element is an array, the value of size tells the dimension of the array. Elements that are not arrays will have a size of one.
4. *Quantity*—for data elements representing aggregates of data (file, record, structure), the entry for quantity is the estimated number of elements (files, records, or structures). Quantity also may be used to represent a second dimension for matrices.
5. *Description*—a brief description of the data. This field may contain range or accuracy information for the data element.

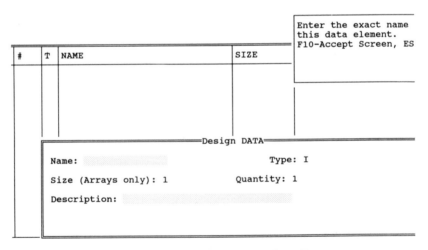

Figure 5.6   Sample CASE Data Entry Form

An example might be illustrative. Suppose we wanted to represent a data file containing aircraft positional information. For each aircraft in the system, we store a call sign (name), a latitude, a longitude, a course, a speed, and an altitude. Figure 5.7 shows how the resulting data structure might be represented by HIPO-II. (This report is generated by *Structured Designer's Toolbox™*.) The column labeled T is a one-letter abbreviation for the data element type.

```
Add   Modify   Delete   Window   Goto   Quit

Add new data element.
```

#	T	NAME	SIZE	QTY
0	DF	Sample	1	1
1	C	⊢Name	30	1
2	F	⊢Latitude	1	1
3	F	⊢Longitude	1	1
4	I	⊢Course	1	1
5	I	⊢Speed	1	1
6	I	└Altitude	1	1

Figure 5.7   Sample Data Structure Representation

5.2 DATA FLOW ANALYSIS WITH HIPO-II

Defining global data structures is only half of the battle. It is equally important that the interfaces between modules in your program be carefully thought out. These interfaces are defined in terms of data flows. Data flows consist of pass parameters (both those used as input and those modified as output), return variables, and global data that is used (input) or modified (output). Careful, comprehensive definition of a program's data flows is critical to the success of a software development project. Data flow information is used as follows:

- Program modules are externally defined strictly in terms of data flows and transformations. This black box view of program modules allows libraries of generic modules to be reused on multiple projects.
- Rigid data flow definitions allow independent development of program modules. As long as each programmer adheres to the specified data flow requirements, integration should proceed smoothly even with little coordination during coding.

- Rigid data flow definitions allow programmers to include common modules in their code before the common modules are even completed.
- Data flows help define a module's functional requirements. For many modules, adequate definition of input and output variables makes the processing requirements self-explanatory.

As with the original HIPO, HIPO-II defines system data flows by describing the input and output variables for each module. This focus on module input and output encourages a black box approach to design. Unlike HIPO, HIPO-II represents this information in a format designed to be identical to that used for module headers normally included in the final source code as internal documentation. The goal is to have a simplified part of the external documentation become the program internal documentation.

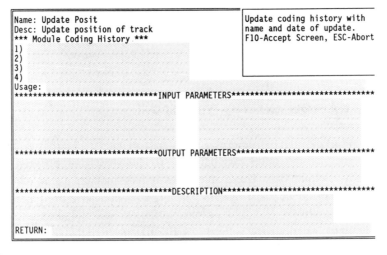

Figure 5.8   Sample HIPO-II Input-Process Data Entry Screen

Figure 5.8 shows a sample HIPO-II data entry screen used to define a module's input and output variables. The small box in the upper right corner is a field-specific prompt that will change as the designer's data entry cursor is moved from field to field. The displayed fields have the following meanings:

- *Name*—The name of the module. The module name was entered during the process of functional decomposition and is displayed here for reference only.

- **Desc**—A brief module description. Once again, this information was entered during the process of functional decomposition and is displayed here for reference only.
- **Module Coding History**—These four fields show the coding history of the module (see Fig. 5.9). Line 1 normally will consist of the initials of the systems analyst and the date the module was defined. Lines 2 through 4 will contain the initials of each person making changes to the module definition, the date of the change, and the reason for the change.

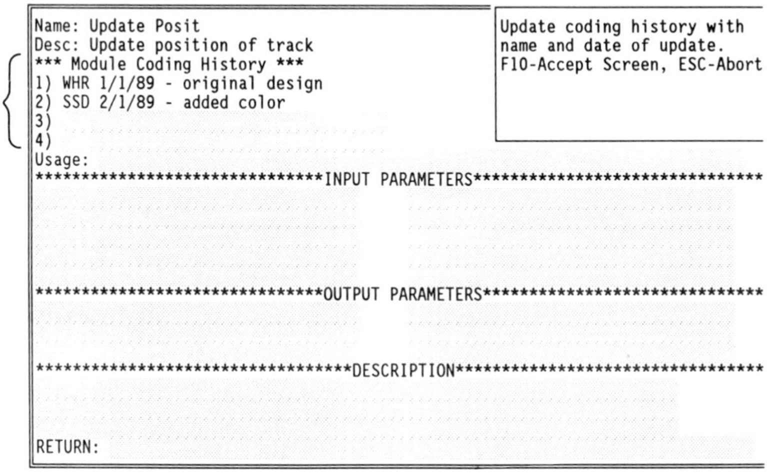

```
Name: Update Posit                              Update coding history with
Desc: Update position of track                  name and date of update.
*** Module Coding History ***                   F10-Accept Screen, ESC-Abort
1) WHR 1/1/89 - original design
2) SSD 2/1/89 - added color
3)
4)
Usage:
****************************INPUT PARAMETERS********************************



****************************OUTPUT PARAMETERS******************************



****************************DESCRIPTION************************************


RETURN:
```

Figure 5.9   Module Coding History

- **Usage**—This field contains a one-line example of how the module is called in normal use (see Fig. 5.10). All parameters that are explicitly passed to or from the module are included, along with their type. (The example shown is for the C programming language.)

```
Name: Update Posit                          Enter a usage line.  Ex.
Desc: Update position of track              'int fseek(FILE *stream,
*** Module Coding History ***               long offset, int
1) WHR 1/1/89 - original design             fromwhere)'
2) SSD 2/1/89 - added color                 F10-Accept Screen, ESC-Abort
3)
4)
Usage: int update_posit(int track_id, int time_duration);
***************************INPUT PARAMETERS*******************************



***************************OUTPUT PARAMETERS*****************************


***************************DESCRIPTION***********************************



RETURN:
```

Figure 5.10   Usage Line

- *Input Parameters*—These 10 fields (6 are used in Fig. 5.11) show all input parameters used by this module. Parameters include variables passed explicitly and global data used by the module. Global data should match data defined in the HIPO-II data hierarchy, and passed parameters should be defined on the usage line of this form. Each entry contains the parameter name followed by a semicolon. If a module has more than 10 input parameters, multiple parameters can be defined in one field.

```
Name: Update Posit                          Enter a three line module
Desc: Update position of track              description.
*** Module Coding History ***               F10-Accept Screen, ESC-Abort
1) WHR 1/1/89 - original design
2) SSD 2/1/89 - added color
3)
4)
Usage: int update_posit(int track_id, int time_duration);
***************************INPUT PARAMETERS*******************************
int track_id;                               int speed;
int time_duration;  --in minutes
float lat; --from file
float long;
int course;
***************************OUTPUT PARAMETERS*****************************


***************************DESCRIPTION***********************************



RETURN:
```

Figure 5.11   Input Parameters

Multiple parameters are separated by commas and terminated by a semicolon. Space in the field following the semicolon contains freeform comments, which may include range information, accuracy requirements, or a brief description of the parameter.

- *Output Parameters*—These six fields show all output parameters of this module (see Fig. 5.12). Parameters include variables returned explicitly and global data modified by the module. The format for each field is identical to that for input parameters (above).

```
Name: Update Posit                          Enter a three line module
Desc: Update position of track              description.
*** Module Coding History ***               F10-Accept Screen, ESC-Abort
1) WHR 1/1/89 - original design
2) SSD 2/1/89 - added color
3)
4)
Usage: int update_posit(int track_id, int time_duration);
*************************INPUT PARAMETERS********************************
int track_id;                     int speed;
int time_duration;  --in minutes
float lat; --from file
float long;
int course;
*************************OUTPUT PARAMETERS******************************
float lat; --to file
float long;
int retval;
*************************DESCRIPTION************************************


RETURN:
```

Figure 5.12   Output Parameters

- *Description*—These three fields are used for a freeform description of the module, including limitations (if any) (see Fig. 5.13). Keywords used to assist in categorizing this module in a software library are included here. Module timing, accuracy, and memory allocations may also be included here.

```
Name: Update Posit                              Enter a three line module
Desc: Update position of track                  description.
*** Module Coding History ***                   F10-Accept Screen, ESC-Abort
1) WHR 1/1/89 - original design
2) SSD 2/1/89 - added color
3)
4)
Usage: int update_posit(int track_id, int time_duration);
****************************INPUT PARAMETERS****************************
int track_id;                          int speed;
int time_duration;  --in minutes
float lat; --from file
float long;
int course;
***************************OUTPUT PARAMETERS***************************
float lat; --to file
float long;
int retval;
*****************************DESCRIPTION*******************************
Module updates unit's position in file using current course and
speed.  PIM leg duration is set by time_duration.  New positions are
calculated using Rhumb line calculations.
RETURN:
```

Figure 5.13   Module Description

- **Return**—This field is used to describe any return parameters, including error codes, if applicable (see Fig. 5.14).

```
Name: Update Posit                              Describe the return value,
Desc: Update position of track                  if appropriate.
*** Module Coding History ***                   F10-Accept Screen, ESC-Abort
1) WHR 1/1/89 - original design
2) SSD 2/1/89 - added color
3)
4)
Usage: int update_posit(int track_id, int time_duration);
****************************INPUT PARAMETERS****************************
int track_id;                          int speed;
int time_duration;  --in minutes
float lat; --from file
float long;
int course;
***************************OUTPUT PARAMETERS***************************
float lat; --to file
float long;
int retval;
*****************************DESCRIPTION*******************************
Module updates unit's position in file using current course and
speed.  PIM leg duration is set by time_duration.  New positions are
calculated using Rhumb line calculations.
RETURN: int retval; 0 = success, -1 for error
```

Figure 5.14   Return Values

Using this format to describe a module's input and output variables offers the following advantages over the original HIPO-II technique:

1. HIPO-II documentation can be automatically downloaded to disk files for use by the programming team. The external input-output variable definitions become the internal source code documentation with no additional data entry.
2. The module input-output definitions are expressed in a format easily understood by programmers and end users. The definitions produced by HIPO-II also match definitions commonly found for library routines and system calls.
3. The HIPO-II format is suitable for automatic data flow verification using CASE tools. Global variable references can be matched against the HIPO-II data hierarchy. Parameters passed between modules can be validated for consistency.
4. Input-output variable definitions can be entered easily and modified on a computer screen.

5.3 SUMMARY

HIPO-II represents data in terms of global data structures and data flows. Global data structures include external files, global internal structures, and global variables. Global data structures are represented hierarchically, and may be used by any program module without being explicitly passed.

Data flow is represented in terms of input and output parameters. Input and output parameters may be passed/returned explicitly or may be global. Input and output parameters are represented in HIPO-II in a standard module header format identical to that used for program module internal documentation. The module header also includes the module description, coding history, sample usage line, and return parameter definitions.

```
┌──────────┐
│ chapter  │
│    6     │
└──────────┘
```

INTERFACES
to
PROJECT
MANAGEMENT

6.1 WORKING WITH PROJECT MANAGEMENT

The HIPO-II method of representing a program design is closely matched to the project work breakdown structure (WBS). A WBS is a hierarchically structured decomposition of the project into tasks. A HIPO-II program design is a hierarchically structured decomposition of the program into program modules and functions. The HIPO-II program decomposition can be easily mapped to specific tasks in the project WBS. For a more complete understanding of project management in general and work breakdown structures in particular, see my book, *Structured Computer Project Management*, (Prentice Hall, 1988).

On the majority of the projects I am familiar with, the project manager and systems analyst are doing only part of their job. The project manager prepares his project plan with little technical input, then cannot understand why

1. It is impossible to determine which work breakdown structure (WBS) element the programmer's time should be charged to because his actual work either does not appear on the WBS or is spread across multiple WBS elements.
2. During most of the project, many WBS elements are started but few WBS elements are fully completed.
3. It is difficult to make cost-benefit trade-offs and risk-reduction plans, often resulting in important design changes being made at the last minute by the programming team.
4. The project is late and over budget.

The systems analyst prepares his program design with little management input, then cannot understand why

1. The project team is forced to account for time based on a totally illogical and meaningless WBS.
2. The large number of modules completed to date is not recognized by the project manager.
3. The project manager and customer are not more clear about what their real priorities are.
4. The project manager never budgets enough time and money to do the job.

The fact is that effective project management requires that the project plan be intimately linked to the program design. A project manager **cannot** do an adequate job without detailed information about the program design. This information includes not only the basic design documentation (already discussed), but specific estimates of resource requirements and risk. On most project teams, this information must come from the technical leader—the systems analyst! Let's look at how lack of communication between these two individuals lead to the above four problems:

---

1. Little relationship between WBS tasks (charge numbers) and actual work performed.

All project managers will insist that project time be tracked against work breakdown structure (WBS) elements. This is necessary to track expenditures versus budgets, both of which are reported to senior management in terms of WBS elements. If the systems analyst does not supply a workable hierarchy for use in the WBS, the project manager will design a WBS that usually will not correspond to the functional decomposition in the program design. Some program functional areas were not included in the WBS because the project manager did not have the technical background to plan for those tasks. Some program function areas are included in several WBS tasks because the project manager did not have the technical background to maintain proper functional cohesion between WBS elements. The end result is a mess when trying to match work performed against WBS elements.

---

2. Project tracking is in terms of WBS elements fully completed, yet few are completed until late in the project.

Because one WBS element includes pieces of many program functional elements, WBS elements are never completed during the project. There is always another program module that must be finished before stating that the WBS element is really done. If the WBS had a one-to-one relationship with the program design, then completed program modules would show up as completed WBS elements. The systems analyst must recognize that management tracks project progress in terms of completed WBS elements, **not** in terms of completed program modules.

---

3. Customers and managers are not able to make effective cost-benefit trade-off decisions.

Cost estimates are prepared and presented for WBS elements, not for program functional areas. If the WBS elements are a poor reflection of the program's functional decomposition, the cost estimates will not be expressed clearly in terms of incremental costs for added functional capabilities. If the customer wants to see the cost savings from deleting a program feature, several affected WBS elements must each be re-estimated. This makes cost-benefit analysis extremely difficult. If we could ensure a one-to-one mapping between program functional modules and WBS elements, and perform cost estimates for each functional module/WBS element, we would know exactly what each program feature costs. This explicit cost per feature information is what the customers need to clarify their priorities.

---

4. Cost and schedule estimates are not adequate.

Because the WBS structure is not very meaningful to the systems analyst, the systems analyst cannot properly provide input about resource requirements (cost and time). Because the program functional design does not map very well to the WBS structure, the project manager cannot adequately communicate budgeted costs per program functional module. The end result is poorly thought out cost estimates, unrealistic budgets, and project problems that do not show up until it is clear that time and/or money is about to run out.

The real problem is simply communication. Neither the project manager nor the systems analyst can do their job properly without close coordination with the other. Figure 6.1 illustrates the tightly coupled nature of the relationship between these two professionals. Many program design techniques produce documentation that simply is not suited for use by the project manager to accomplish his job. The resulting mismatch between the management view of the project and the technical view of the project results in the problems just described. The solution is to select a design technique that facilitates the communication between the project manager and the systems analyst.

To fully understand the project manager's job, you might wish to read my book *Structured Computer Project Management* (Prentice-Hall, 1988). This chapter clarifies the working relation between you as

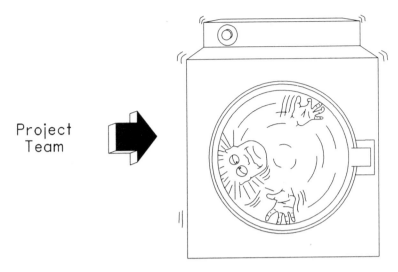

Figure 6.1   You're All in This Together

a systems analyst and your project manager. I will describe how HIPO-II fits into this relationship and facilitates the flow of information between both parties. Figure 6.2 summarizes the top-level data flows between the project manager and the systems analyst. Data elements fall into the following four categories:

1. Hierarchical structure
2. Cost-estimating and design to cost trade-offs
3. Risk estimates and reduction strategies
4. Schedule inputs

Each of these four categories will be described in more detail in the remainder of this chapter.

6.2 HIERARCHICAL STRUCTURE

The project WBS forms the basis of all management-related planning. On projects of any significant size, it is not possible to prepare a detailed WBS at the beginning of the project. There is simply not sufficient information available. The solution most project managers use is to prepare the WBS in stages, with each stage adding more detail. As shown in Fig. 6.3, project managers prepare the WBS in three stages during a typical project:

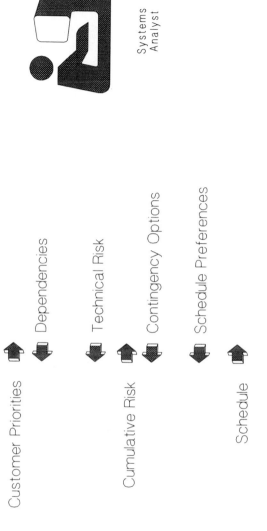

Allocated Resources

Schedule Restrictions

Program Design Hierarchy

WBS

Resource Estimates

Dependencies

Customer Priorities

Technical Risk

Cumulative Risk

Contingency Options

Schedule Preferences

Schedule

Systems Analyst

Project Manager

Figure 6.2 Project Manager–Systems Analyst Data Flows

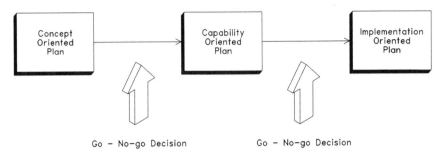

Go – No-go Decision   Go – No-go Decision

Figure 6.3   Three Stages of Planning

1. **Concept Oriented Planning:** A top-level WBS based on broad requirements and management objectives is prepared, normally before a contract for the work is awarded. The concept-oriented WBS is designed to estimate the scope of the work in terms of technical performance, cost, and schedule. Figure 6.4 shows a sample WBS generated as part of the concept-oriented planning.

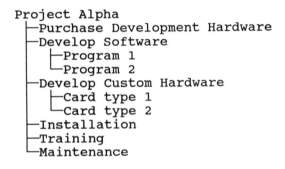

```
Project Alpha
   ├─Purchase Development Hardware
   ├─Develop Software
   │    ├─Program 1
   │    └─Program 2
   ├─Develop Custom Hardware
   │    ├─Card type 1
   │    └─Card type 2
   ├─Installation
   ├─Training
   └─Maintenance
```

Figure 6.4   Sample Concept-Oriented WBS

2. **Function Oriented Planning:** After the contract is awarded, a function-oriented WBS is prepared. The function-oriented decomposition expands the software elements of the concept-oriented plan to include a breakdown of program functionality from the user's perspective. This breakdown corresponds to the initial hierarchy of menu, keyboard, and interrupt modules described in Chapter 2. Figure 6.5 shows a sample hierarchical decomposition generated as part of the function-oriented planning.

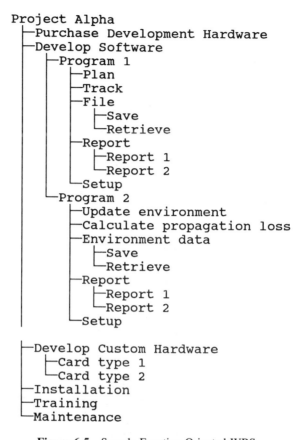

```
Project Alpha
 ├─Purchase Development Hardware
 ├─Develop Software
 │   ├─Program 1
 │   │   ├─Plan
 │   │   ├─Track
 │   │   ├─File
 │   │   │   ├─Save
 │   │   │   └─Retrieve
 │   │   ├─Report
 │   │   │   ├─Report 1
 │   │   │   └─Report 2
 │   │   └─Setup
 │   └─Program 2
 │       ├─Update environment
 │       ├─Calculate propagation loss
 │       ├─Environment data
 │       │   ├─Save
 │       │   └─Retrieve
 │       ├─Report
 │       │   ├─Report 1
 │       │   └─Report 2
 │       └─Setup
 │
 ├─Develop Custom Hardware
 │   ├─Card type 1
 │   └─Card type 2
 ├─Installation
 ├─Training
 └─Maintenance
```

Figure 6.5   Sample Function-Oriented WBS

3. **Implementation Oriented Planning:** As the design is completed, an implementation-oriented WBS is prepared. The implementation-oriented decomposition expands the functional decomposition to include internal program modules to be developed or integrated. These modules correspond to the processing, common, and library modules described in Chapter 2. Figure 6.6 shows a sample hierarchical decomposition generated as part of the implementation-oriented planning.

It should be clear that the project manager is almost totally dependent on the systems analyst for generation of the detailed portions of the function-oriented decomposition and implementation-oriented decomposition. If the project WBS does not track with the software design, it is a failure on the part of both the project manager

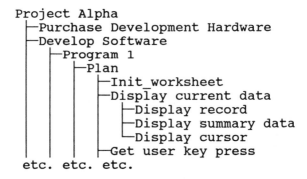

Figure 6.6   Sample Implementation-Oriented WBS

and the systems analyst. HIPO-II hierarchical decompositions are specifically designed to facilitate this vital communication link.

Using HIPO-II, the systems analyst begins by designing the program menu structure, special key handling, and interrupt processing capabilities. This functional hierarchy is reviewed with both the customer and the project manager. The project manager and systems analyst work together to prepare cost and risk estimates for each functional area. If the cost and risk are acceptable, the user-oriented functional hierarchy forms the basis of a contractual commitment to the customer as well as a planning and tracking tool for the project team.

As the systems analyst designs the program internal structure necessary to provide the functional capabilities, the user-oriented functional hierarchy is expanded with processing, common, and library modules. When the internal design is sufficiently advanced to allow implementation to begin, these implementation-oriented modules are provided to the project manager. Once again, cost and risk are estimated and specific modules scheduled for coding and testing.

In summary, HIPO-II program hierarchies are designed to closely match project management WBS hierarchies. The user-oriented designs (menu, keyboard, and internal) are available early in the design process, represent a delivery commitment in a format acceptable to most customers, and allow explicit cost-benefit analysis to be performed for specific program features. As internal modules (process, common, and library) are added to the program functional hierarchy, these form lower level WBS elements for use by the project manager. Project cost estimates are more accurate and meaningful, schedules use actual program modules that must be implemented and tested, and project tracking is meaningful.

6.3 COST ESTIMATING AND DESIGN TO COST TRADE-OFFS

We showed how a one-to-one mapping between the WBS and the program functional hierarchy can lead to more meaningful cost estimates, and alluded to the fact that cost estimates are prepared *throughout* the project, not just during the initial stages. One common misconception about resource estimates is that the initial estimates prepared during the concept-oriented plan are the only important estimates, and that resource estimation at later scheduling stages is a waste of time because "the project budget is already fixed in concrete." This false logic ignores the critical fact that estimates prepared during later stages of software planning are *always* more accurate than earlier estimates. These later estimates can be used to validate earlier estimates, or to point out cost-related problems in the project.

If the estimates point out a problem with earlier estimates, three alternatives are available to the project manager (see Fig. 6.7):

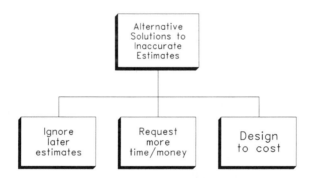

Figure 6.7   Alternatives When Early Estimates are Wrong

1. Later, more accurate estimates can be ignored. This alternative results in the common problem of cost overruns occurring at the later stages of the project and almost always results in a high degree of customer dissatisfaction.
2. Earlier estimates can be revised and additional funds from the customer requested. If the customer understands the fact that estimates prepared during the concept-oriented planning stage are only accurate within plus or minus 50 percent, this option might be reasonable. In any event, it is always better for the

customer to be apprised of this type of news as early as possible (as opposed to waiting until the project actually does run out of money).

3. Finally, the function- or implementation-based cost estimates can be used to revise the design to match the original estimates. This "design to cost" approach is extremely effective under these circumstances both because the precise causes of high costs are clearly understood and because it is early enough in the project for something to be done about the problem.

Because the systems analyst is a key player on the cost-estimating team, it is important that you understand the estimating process from the project manager's perspective. Resource estimation for software development tasks is normally a two-step process (see Fig. 6.8). First, the man power required to perform each task is estimated. These man power estimates are normally based on a category of labor (senior programmer, systems analyst, etc.) and are expressed in man-hours. Man power estimates normally assume an optimal task duration, that is, the implementor will have plenty of time to perform the work in an efficient manner. Resource estimates normally are expressed as an optimistic estimate, a most likely estimate, and a pessimistic estimate so that the project manager can determine the standard deviation for the estimate. This is the information that the systems analyst should prepare and provide to the project manager for each stage of planning. The project manager will convert the resource estimates into dollar amounts. If the project cost is too large, the project manager either will request additional funds from the customer or else work with the systems analyst to modify the design to fit within the available funds. The process of modifying the design to match available funds must be an interactive process between the systems analyst and the project manager.

Second, the resource estimates are used to determine the optimal calendar time required to implement each identified task. If external

Figure 6.8   Resource Estimation

constraints force the schedule to be accelerated, the resource estimates can be increased, the likelihood of success can be reduced, or a combination of the two may be required. This analysis is conducted by the project manager using standard formulas and algorithms (see my book, *Structured Computer Project Management,* Prentice-Hall, 1988).

6.4 RISK ESTIMATES AND REDUCTION STRATEGIES

You will often be required to assist in project risk planning. Project managers will want to perform a detailed risk analysis for the following four reasons:

1. Resources (time, money, and management attention) can be allocated based on each task's risk.
2. Candidate tasks for prototyping can be identified. Prototyping software functions or modules is often the most powerful method available to reduce overall project risk.
3. A risk-optimized schedule can be generated. A risk-optimized schedule attempts to schedule risky tasks as early as possible in the project to allow sufficient time for recovery in the event of failure.
4. Contingency planning is possible.

It is useful to understand some of the risk-related terms that you may be required to estimate. Software development projects typically have four types of risk associated with each task: (1) network risk; (2) technical risk; (3) schedule risk; and (4) cost risk. For each of these types of task-related risk, the project manager will want to determine the task's overall Task Risk Factor (R_t). This will often involve first calculating the Likelihood of Failure Factor (L_f), and Consequence of Failure Factor (C_f). Figure 6.9 summarizes this process.

Calculating Network Risk Components

Network risk involves risk related to the dependency network linking various project tasks. Looking at Fig. 6.10, it is intuitively obvious that Task five in Project one has much less network risk than Task five in Project two. For software tasks, the project manager will

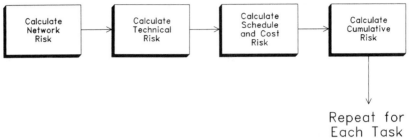

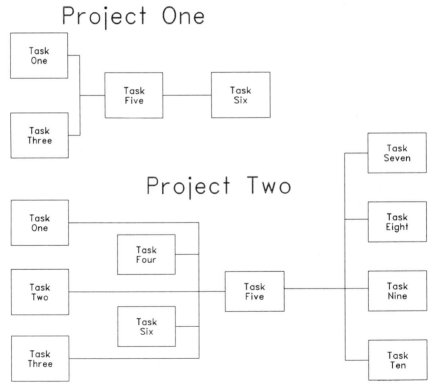

Figure 6.9   Process of Risk Analysis

rely on the systems analyst for input about each task's predecessors and successors (dependencies). These are defined as follows:

> *Predecessor Tasks*—all tasks that must be at least partially completed prior to this task starting
>
> *Successor Tasks*—all tasks that have this task as a predecessor

Figure 6.10   Network Risk

The project manager will use the number of predecessor tasks to determine a task's probability of failure component of network risk. The number of successor tasks will be used to determine a task's consequence of failure component of network risk. These two numbers will be combined to determine the task's network risk.

Calculating Technical Risk Components

A task's technical risk analysis looks at the risk associated with a failure to complete the task to a required degree of technical excellence. For example, a parallel port line driver that must operate at 9600 bytes per second would be a technical failure if the code could not be made to handle the appropriate data rates. Note that this would be a technical failure even if the module was completed on time and on budget. To calculate each task's technical task risk factor, the project manager will first calculate the technical likelihood of failure and consequence of failure factors. These calculations are made based on input from the systems analyst.

A task's technical likelihood of failure factor is a number between one and ten representing your estimate of how likely the task is to miss its technical goals, even with a reasonable cost or schedule overrun. As shown in Fig. 6.11, the likelihood of failure factor for software development tasks is best estimated by independently examining the following four potential causes of technical failure:

1. M_h—The likelihood of failure due to the immaturity of the hardware technology

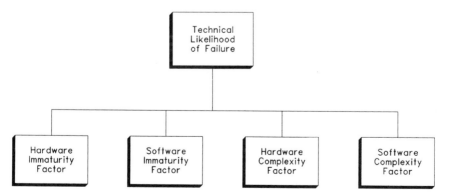

Figure 6.11   Components of Technical Likelihood of Failure

2. M_s—The likelihood of failure due to the immaturity of the software technology

3. C_h—The likelihood of failure due to the complexity of the system's hardware

4. C_s—The likelihood of failure due to the complexity of the system's software

Figure 6.12 presents a table with some general guidelines for assigning a likelihood of failure estimate for each of these four factors. The task's final likelihood of failure factor can be obtained by averaging the four factors just described. A task's technical consequence of failure factor is a number between one and ten that represents your estimate of how serious a task failure will be in a technical sense. The table shown in Fig. 6.13 can be used to determine each task's consequence of failure factor. The project manager will use these two factors to calculate each task's overall technical risk factor.

Calculating Schedule Risk Components

Based on external schedule constraints and customer/management willingness to accept schedule risk, each task is assigned a duration. These durations are compared to the optimum task duration (based on resource requirements) to determine the schedule risk for the project. These calculations use standard formulas and do not normally require input from the systems analyst.

Calculating Cost Risk Components

As mentioned earlier, your estimates for each task's resource requirements will be expressed as an optimistic estimate, a most likely estimate (the mode), and a pessimistic estimate. The project manager will use these three numbers to determine the mean value for resource requirements and the standard deviation. This information is then used to calculate the task's cost risk component.

Value	M_h	M_s	C_h	C_s		
1	Existing	Existing	Simple Design	Simple Design		
3	Minor Redesign	Minor Redesign	Somewhat Complex	Somewhat Complex		
5	Major Change Feasible	Major Change Feasible	Moderate Complexity	Moderate Complexity		
7	Complex Design	New Software	Significant Complexity	Significant Complexity		
9	State of the Art	State of the Art	Extremely Complex	Extremely Complex		

Figure 6.12 Likelihood of Failure Value Guidelines

Value	Technical	Cost	Schedule
1	Minimal Consequences	Within budget	Negligible slip
3	Small reduction in performance	Cost increase of 1 to 10 percent	Minor slip
5	Moderate reduction in performance	Cost increase of 10 to 25 percent	Moderate slip
7	Significant reduction in performance	Cost increase of 25 to 50 percent	Significant slip
9	Technical goals might not be achievable	Cost increase over 50 percent	Unacceptable slip

Figure 6.13 Consequence of Failure Factor Guidelines

6.5 SCHEDULE INPUTS

A software schedule is measured in terms of its time, cost, and risk. Ideally, the project manager would like to produce a schedule that is optimal for all three variables, but this is never possible. For example, a software development schedule can be produced which accelerates development tremendously (optimum in terms of time), but this always will cost more than development at a more orderly pace. It is possible to produce a schedule that is optimal in terms of any one of the variables, at the expense of the other two, but this is only done in unusual circumstances. For example, a crash program to produce software under emergency circumstances might trade high risk of failure and high cost for a potential delivery in record time.

On most projects, an acceptable limit for two of the variables is selected and the schedule is optimized in terms of the third variable while holding the other two at their acceptable value. Other variables that might act as limiting factors during software scheduling are

- Required calendar completion dates
- Cash-flow restrictions
- Limited resources, especially people
- Required administrative time to obtain approvals

During scheduling, the project manager will be using the following five guidelines:

1. Tasks must not be scheduled in conflict with their dependency definitions. If task one must be complete prior to starting task two, the schedule must reflect this dependency. Software task dependencies are defined with significant input from the systems analyst.

2. Tasks should not be scheduled to require more resources during any given week than will be available. Resources might include terminal hours, specific individuals or categories of labor, or cash. Inputs from the systems analyst regarding task resource requirements obviously provide the information needed to achieve this goal.

3. The project manager will attempt to minimize parallel assignments of people. People work most efficiently when they can

concentrate on one task at a time. With a well designed WBS and assistance from the systems analyst, this normally is possible.

4. Tasks should be scheduled to maximize resource leveling. Resource leveling is defined as moving tasks to minimize fluctuations from week to week in required resource levels. It is obviously preferable to have 10 programmers working on the project from week one through 20 rather than having 30 programmers required for the first five weeks, none for the next 10 weeks, and 10 programmers required for the last five weeks. The project manager will perform resource leveling using the task resource requirements determined by the systems analyst.

5. The project manager will attempt to maximize resource cohesion. Resource cohesion is a measure of the uniformity of the type of work individual programmers are assigned to do during the project. If four port drivers and four report formatting modules must be written by two programmers, resource cohesion would be maximized by assigning one programmer to write the four drivers and the second programmer to write the four report formatting modules. This clearly is to be preferred over a plan that had each programmer write two drivers and two report formatters. Because the systems analyst has the most clear idea of each module's contents, significant inputs are necessary to assist the project manager in maximizing resource cohesion.

Within the above five guidelines, an overall implementation strategy is still necessary. On most projects, the systems analyst will play a key role in the scheduling of specific program modules for implementation. As a programmer, I preferred bottom-up programming. The most difficult code normally was at the bottom of the hierarchy, so bottom-up coding got the hard part done first. I generally had a clear idea of the structure of the low-level code prior to completion of the high-level design, so bottom-up development allowed me to begin low-level coding work in parallel with final design work.

As a manager, I preferred top-down programming. The software was operational within a few weeks of the start of coding, with stubs in place of modules not yet developed. Partial implementation and delivery, in order of customer priority, was simple. Perhaps best of all, there were no last-minute surprises trying to integrate a program that simply did not fit together.

As my experience increased, I became convinced that both methods had their strengths, yet neither was perfect. There had to be a better way! After extensive experimentation in the real world, I can emphatically state that the optimum method of developing software is a combination of top down and bottom up, as shown in Fig. 6.14. The approach is beautiful in its simplicity, and I will describe it here.

Bottom-Up Component

Bottom-up coding work should be performed by junior programmers and senior programmers who are not capable of acting as lead programmers (that is, technical programmers with a very narrow focus). Four types of modules are candidates for bottom-up programming:

1. Modules that have a high degree of risk (technical, network, cost, or schedule). These should be coded early to allow time to recover in the event of failure.

2. Modules that are expected to require a long development time relative to the available time for software development. These

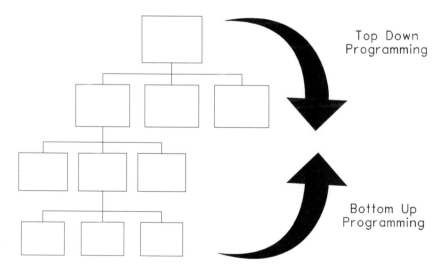

Figure 6.14   Bottom-Up and Top-Down Programming

should be started early so that schedule slips will not delay final delivery.

3. Modules that are used in many locations within your program hierarchy (common modules).

4. Modules that will require extensive, time-consuming testing to verify proper operation. These should be started early to allow sufficient time for adequate testing.

Top-Down Component

All modules not meeting the criteria for bottom-up coding, including most processing modules in the program hierarchy, should be coded in a top-down fashion. This programming should be the responsibility of the lead programmer, assisted as required by other less senior programmers. Top-down programming basically involves coding modules starting at the top of the hierarchy and working down, using stubs for modules that do not exist yet.

There are two approaches to top-down coding that are in common use: breadth first top-down coding, and depth first top-down coding, also called threaded top-down coding. These two methods are illustrated in Fig. 6.15. Breadth first top-down coding requires that each

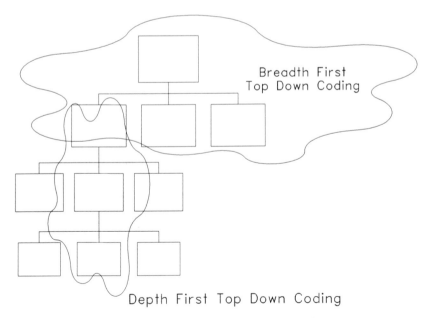

Figure 6.15   Breadth First versus Depth First Top-Down Coding

level of the program hierarchy be completed prior to proceeding to the next lower level. This method is favored by theorists, who provide convincing evidence that it is the only way of producing provably correct programs. I find this method is appropriate for the first one or two levels of the processing modules and for the entire user interface portion of the hierarchy (menu, key, and interrupt modules).

Depth first, or threaded, top-down coding involves coding all modules required to implement, test, and demonstrate one program function at a time. After one program function is satisfactorily completed, the next function is started. This often can be accomplished by implementing one user menu function at a time. Depth first top-down coding is favored by real world software developers who are constantly under the gun to "show us something that works". I favor depth first top-down coding for all processing modules below the second or third tier of the program hierarchy. Figure 6.16 summarizes my recommended approach to scheduling program implementation.

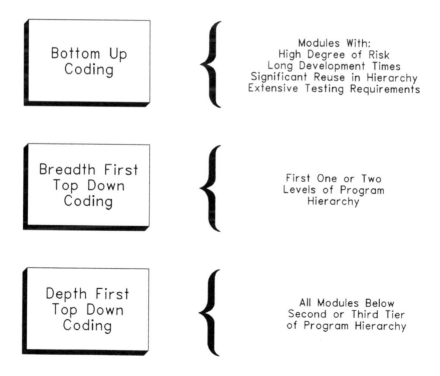

Figure 6.16   Recommended Approach to Program Implementation

6.6 SUMMARY

As systems analyst, your job includes extensive coordination with the project manager. You should work with the project manager to ensure that the project detailed WBS accurately reflects your program functional decomposition. For each functional element, you should provide estimates of cost, risk, and dependencies. If necessary, work with the project manager to modify the design and reduce cost and/or risk. Work with the project manager to generate a schedule that is logical in terms of the program's functional hierarchy. In many ways, these efforts contribute as much to the eventual success of the overall project as do your design efforts.

chapter 7

TRANSITION
to
CODING

We've all heard the horror stories about software development projects that tried to skip the design stage. By rushing to implement a poorly thought out design, the project failed in a spectacular fashion. As a new systems analyst, I was determined that this would never happen to me. My first real project involved approximately $50,000 worth of work. Using the latest in software design techniques, I completed the design. In reviewing the work, I decided that it needed more refinement. After completing these changes, I thought about it some more and decided that still more improvements were possible. This process continued until, much to my surprise, I had spent almost $40,000 of the available money. I had a great design and no money or time to implement it! Believe me, the customer was not impressed.

On another occasion, I was project manager for a program to develop a military communication processing application. We completed the design documents to the appropriate military standards and they were accepted by the customer. As we began implementing the software, we discovered that the design could be improved to offer more capability, faster development, and lower cost. These changes involved some restructuring of the program hierarchy and modular decomposition. We proposed the design changes to the customer, but permission to modify the design was refused. The customer explained that it would be too expensive to make the required changes to the design documents. This was a clear case of the design documents hindering, rather than helping, the development effort.

In both cases, the transition from design to coding was flawed. In the first example, the coding stage was delayed too long for effective implementation of the design. In the second example, the transition from design to coding was too abrupt. Figure 7.1 shows the traditional "textbook" view of the relationship between software design and software implementation. Figure 7.2 shows the optimum relationship between software design and software implementation. The programmers and systems analysts work together throughout the project. Early work is almost exclusively performed by systems analysts, with programmers helping by prototyping or modeling some critical areas that affect design decisions. As the project progresses, the role of the systems analyst steadily becomes less significant as the role of the programmer increases. At the end of the project, work is performed almost exclusively by programmers with systems analysts providing insight or clarification when required.

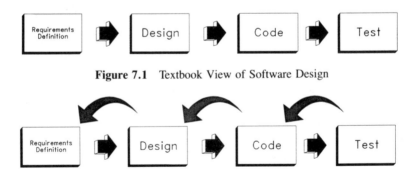

Figure 7.1   Textbook View of Software Design

Figure 7.2   Optimum View of Software Design

7.1 STAGES OF DESIGN

Software design is accomplished in six stages (Fig. 7.3). Early design stages result in formal (legally binding) or informal (not legally binding) contractual commitments to the end user, but little or no input for programmers. As these early stages are completed and firmed up,

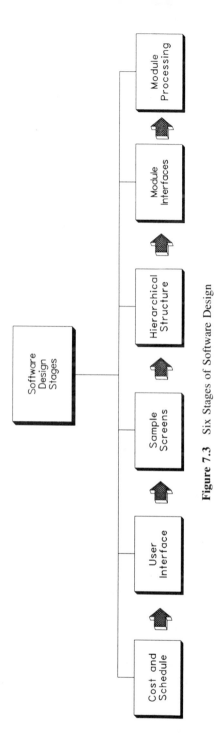

Figure 7.3   Six Stages of Software Design

later stages add detail to the design. This detail allows programmers to begin work during the design process. In this way, initial experience gained during the program coding can be incorporated in the detailed design. Let's clarify this process by discussing each of the six stages of design.

1. **Cost and Schedule:** On many projects, a contract is signed at an early stage in the project life cycle, effectively freezing the cost and schedule. From this point on, all development work is design to cost. Systems analysts should have generalized inputs to the broad commitments and cost estimates prepared as part of this stage of design.

2. **User Interface:** Initial design work focuses on the user-oriented program features, normally described via a menu hierarchy, interrupt processing, and keyboard modules. It is this aspect of the software that the end user is most likely to get heavily involved with during design. The end user is also likely to evaluate the delivery of the final software in terms of implementation of the agreed upon menu hierarchy. End users will notice missing menu options, but are not likely to care about internal changes to the functions that implement the individual options. Systems analysts normally will be the primary authors of the menu structure documentation.

3. **Sample Screens:** With the user interface designed, the end users are likely to turn their attention to the program's user interface (reports and data entry screens). Although changes to the report formats and data entry layouts are possible throughout development, the end users normally will not be comfortable with major changes in this area once the formats have been approved. Because the data entry fields and report information involve the design of data structures and top-level algorithm design, this work is accomplished primarily by the systems analyst with some assistance from programmers as desired.

4. **Hierarchical Structure:** The hierarchical program structure generally is used by project managers to assign work, budget resources, schedule development, and track expenditures. Although the end user usually does not care about the program's internal structure, project managers typically are not happy if the structure changes drastically throughout

development. It is common for the systems analyst to prepare the top-level hierarchical structure and for both the systems analyst and the programmers to prepare parts of the detailed hierarchical structure. When the hierarchical structure is complete, programmers often can begin collecting and modifying existing functions that will be incorporated in this program.

5. **Module Interface Specifications:** Module interface specifications do not affect the end user or the project manager, but have a significant effect on the programmers. Seemingly minor changes in this area can have unexpected results for a different programmer working on a different part of the program hierarchy. Module interface specifications typically will change somewhat throughout development, but the changes will be less and less significant as implementation proceeds simply because too many other modules will be affected. Top-level interface specifications usually are prepared by the systems analyst, while detailed interface specifications are often prepared by the programmers. For modules without complex processing requirements (most modules), coding can begin as the interface specifications are completed.

6. **Module Internal Processing:** Module internal processing only affects that module, as long as the module interface specification is met. Although any changes to the processing must ensure that the module still meets the processing requirements required by its specification, internal processing modifications often are made to modules throughout implementation. Complex or critical internal processing definitions normally are prepared by the systems analyst, but straightforward internal processing definitions generally are prepared by the programmers and approved by the systems analyst.

Many people become quite agitated when presented with this type of software development approach. They point out the fact that configuration control in this fluid environment is difficult, and express fear that the software may degenerate to many individual development efforts that fail to properly integrate together. This objection is reasonable, but can be overcome with appropriate configuration control techniques made easier with HIPO-II.

7.2 CONFIGURATION CONTROL DURING DEVELOPMENT

Few software design teams have sufficient background with a new program being designed to produce an optimum design on their own. A vital element in producing the design is feedback from the end user during early stages of development, and from the programmers during later stages of development. Unfortunately, many design techniques result in design documentation that is difficult or impossible to keep up-to-date in this dynamic environment. Massive wall charts showing all data flows may make impressive wallpaper, but they do little to facilitate production of good designs. The key is to use a design technique that is both easy to maintain and easy to control. HIPO-II meets these requirements.

Using HIPO-II, software designs are easy to maintain. The design is produced in stages, with each stage expanding a new aspect of the program by building on earlier work. The HIPO-II menu, interrupt, and keyboard modules represent the functional design of the program. Adding the processing, library, and common modules completes the detail program design. Within stages, the hierarchical nature of HIPO-II encourages a stepwise decomposition of the problem, each level in the hierarchy expanding the level above (see Fig. 7.4). Finally, the simple representations of the design chosen by HIPO-II facilitate easy modifications as they are required.

Easy maintenance of the software design is a necessary, but not sufficient, condition for success. An all-too-common problem occurs

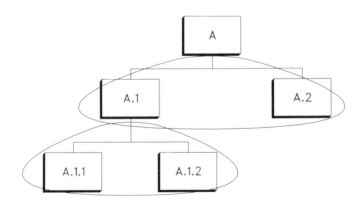

Figure 7.4 Hierarchical Designs Encourage Stepwise Refinement

on large projects when the design is modified—individual project team members work to out-of-date specifications. Sally goes on vacation for the week when the new design updates are released and never finds out about the changes. Joe forgets to pick up the modified design and continues using the old documents. Sue doesn't think the changes will affect her so she never bothers to make the page changes, and so on.

HIPO-II solves this problem by representing the design in a format compatible with a computer terminal. The design is maintained, by one individual or group, on a single disk. As changes are made to the design, this master copy of the design is updated on the disk. If multiple versions are desired, older copies of the design may be archived. If a project team member wishes to view the design, she simply pulls up the appropriate design documentation on her computer terminal. The latest version of the design is always at every team member's fingertips.

In addition to simplifying configuration control of the emerging software design, HIPO-II encourages and facilitates the capture and re-use of existing software and software design. This set of features will be amplified in the following section.

7.3 EFFECTIVE SOFTWARE CAPTURE

Most software engineers will agree that the capture and re-use of existing software is one of the most significant productivity aids available to a software team. After a little thought, it should be clear that it is at least as important to capture existing design work. Although the re-use of software libraries is commonly understood and attempted, the re-use of existing designs is less common. One problem is that most design documents are not designed to allow individual pieces of the design to be removed and re-used. HIPO-II, on the other hand, is specifically designed to allow the design to be segmented, stored in design libraries, and re-used on other projects.

HIPO-II allows a design team to build up a library of hierarchical design components. When using hierarchical elements from the design library, the new project simply inserts the stored design segment. Top-level functions can be included in a new design and will automatically include all detailed supporting levels under the top-level function. If the top-level modules are not directly applicable, lower level modules may be extracted from the library and individually included. When inserting library components, HIPO-II automatically includes the appropriate control flow, header information (input-output), and pseudocode.

Perhaps an example would be illustrative. Suppose we wanted to design a program to monitor tactical information being received over an HF (High Frequency) radio, parse out position updates on contacts, filter the resulting tracks using a Kalman filter, and plot the results. We look at our design library (see Fig. 7.5) and notice that several existing design elements are appropriate. We insert those into our design hierarchy, resulting in a hierarchy as shown in Fig. 7.6. We now must add the new routines to parse out the position information from the received data stream, but we notice that some low-level routines from the library are relevant. We add some new design elements mixed with the existing routines that are useful, resulting in the hierarchy shown in Fig. 7.7. It must be stressed that the resulting design includes not only the hierarchical module names, but also automatically includes all

```
HF Radio Interface
 ├─Monitor port
 │   ├─Control line processing
 │   ├─Data receipt
 │   └─Data buffering
 ├─Baudot to ASCII
 ├─Remove header
 ├─Error processing
 └─EOL sequence conversion

Parse weather messages
 ├─Decompose
 │   ├─Break into lines
 │   └─Break into fields
 ├─Extract current weather
 ├─Extract predicted weather
 └─Update files

Track Filter
 ├─Initialize Kalman filter
 ├─Process update
 └─Adjust paramaters

Plot tracks
 ├─Init display
 ├─Plot background
 ├─Erase track
 └─Draw track
```

Figure 7.5   Design Library Contents

supporting design documentation (header, input-output descriptions, pseudocode, control flow).

In addition to allowing the systems analyst to capture and re-use existing hierarchical design elements, HIPO-II allows you to capture and re-use sample program outputs. Sample screens, data entry forms, overlays, and reports can be saved to disk to build a library of sample outputs. On new projects, these outputs can be inserted into the new design where appropriate. After being inserted, they can be modified, if necessary, to tailor them to the new application.

One side benefit of the HIPO-II representation of program structures is a greatly improved ability to verify and validate the completed software, as we shall see in the following section.

7.4 VERIFICATION AND VALIDATION

Software V&V (verification and validation) is often accomplished in three steps:

1. During development, individual modules and groups of modules are tested to ensure that they perform in accordance with the specifications. This is often called unit testing.

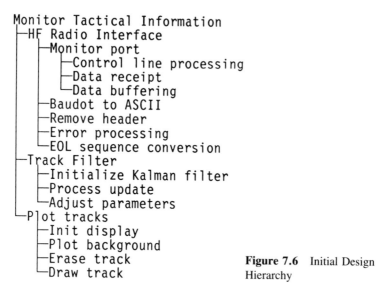

```
Monitor Tactical Information
 ├─HF Radio Interface
 │    ├─Monitor port
 │    │    ├─Control line processing
 │    │    ├─Data receipt
 │    │    └─Data buffering
 │    ├─Baudot to ASCII
 │    ├─Remove header
 │    ├─Error processing
 │    └─EOL sequence conversion
 ├─Track Filter
 │    ├─Initialize Kalman filter
 │    ├─Process update
 │    └─Adjust parameters
 └─Plot tracks
      ├─Init display
      ├─Plot background
      ├─Erase track
      └─Draw track
```

Figure 7.6   Initial Design Hierarchy

```
Monitor Tactical Information
├─HF Radio Interface
│   ├─Monitor port
│   │   ├─Control line processing
│   │   ├─Data receipt
│   │   └─Data buffering
│   ├─Baudot to ASCII
│   ├─Remove header
│   ├─Error processing
│   └─EOL sequence conversion
├─Track Filter
│   ├─Initialize Kalman filter
│   ├─Process update
│   └─Adjust parameters
├─Parse Track Data
│   ├─Decompose
│   │   ├─Break into lines
│   │   └─Break into fields
│   ├─Extract position
│   └─Update structures
└─Plot tracks
    ├─Init display
    ├─Plot background
    ├─Erase track
    └─Draw track


Parse weather messages
├─Decompose
│   ├─Break into lines
│   └─Break into fields
├─Extract current weather
├─Extract predicted weather
└─Update files

Track Filter
├─Initialize Kalman filter
├─Process update
└─Adjust parameters

Plot tracks
├─Init display
├─Plot background
├─Erase track
└─Draw track
```

Figure 7.7   Final Design Hierarchy

2. As all modules necessary to accomplish a specific functional task are completed, the performance of these functional tasks is verified. This is called threaded or depth first system level testing.

3. After the entire system is completed, system level testing verifies that integration has been performed properly and that module interactions do not have unexpected side effects. This is called top-level system testing.

Because specific program modules can be traced to specific descriptions in the program design hierarchy, unit testing is simple. The inputs and outputs are explained in the module's header (input-output) description. Processing requirements are explained in the header's description and in the module's pseudocode. The module's performance in accordance with these requirements can be verified easily.

With HIPO-II, functional tasks correspond to program hierarchy modules of type menu, interrupt, or keyboard. With threaded system level testing, each of these functional tasks will be verified individually. Each thread can be tested when all modules below it in the program design hierarchy have been completed. This allows threaded system level testing (and demonstration) to be accomplished as the program is being implemented. This approach also simplifies scheduling to complete high priority threads as early as possible (simply schedule implementation of all modules under the high priority thread). Verification is accomplished using the module's description and input-output definition, as with unit testing.

System level testing normally involves repeating the test of each functional thread after the software is fully integrated. The testing team is looking for unexpected changes in the test results due to module interactions and for significant performance problems in the fully integrated system.

7.5 SUMMARY

HIPO-II supports a stepwise refinement of the software design both by supporting multiple stages of design and by supporting hierarchical decomposition within each stage. On-line maintenance of design documentation helps to simplify modifications of the design and ensures that the project team always knows where to find the latest version of the design. The modular, black box design approach of HIPO-II, combined with CASE tools for inserting and extracting design components to disk, facilitates the capture and re-use of design elements from previous projects. Finally, software verification and validation at the unit, threaded function, and system level are simplified by validating the code against readily identified components of the HIPO-II design.

chapter 8

COMPARISON of HIPO-II with OTHER DESIGN TECHNIQUES

In this chapter, we will provide a framework for evaluations of HIPO-II against six other common design techniques:

1. Structured Analysis and Design Technique (SADT)
2. Jackson Methodology (JM)
3. Warnier-Orr Methodology (WOM)
4. Higher Order Software (HOS)
5. HIPO (original version)
6. Nassi-Shneiderman charts (NS)

I assume that the reader is familiar with each of these techniques. If necessary, you may refer to the book *Diagramming Techniques for Analysts and Programmers* by James Martin and Corma McClure (Prentice-Hall, 1985).

To perform the evaluation, we will use a value-contribution model approach. This basically involves dividing the evaluation into individual criteria and subcriteria and assigning a relative weight to each criterion and subcriterion. The relative weight represents how important that particular criterion is to your organization. Each technique to be evaluated is then rated on a scale of 1 (low) to 10 (high) in each of the identified areas. Finally, the absolute scores are adjusted using the relative weights to arrive at a final value contribution. Don't worry if this process is not clear. As you follow the analysis in this chapter, the value-contribution approach to comparison should become clear.

8.1 FIVE DIMENSIONS OF EVALUATION

As we discussed earlier in this book, design techniques must be evaluated from the perspective of all project participants, not just from the perspective of the systems analyst. As shown in Fig. 8.1, we will perform the evaluation in the following five dimensions:

1. *Manager*—compatibility with project management goals and requirements
2. *User*—usefulness in facilitating the user-developer team approach to design
3. *Programmer*—value to the program implementor
4. *Systems Analyst*—suitability for continuous use by the systems analyst
5. *CASE*—compatibility with CASE limitations imposed by affordable computer hardware

As discussed above, we will use a value-contribution approach to evaluating the various design techniques. For each of the five areas, we will describe relevant evaluation criteria and score each technique versus each criterion. We will then estimate the perceived importance (value) of each criterion and use these numbers to determine the weighted values for each technique. Finally, we will estimate the perceived importance of each dimension and use these numbers to determine the weighted values for each technique across all dimensions. This process is summarized in Fig. 8.2.

The value-contribution model can be tailored easily to your company. Simply review the relative weights of each evaluation criterion and adjust as desired.

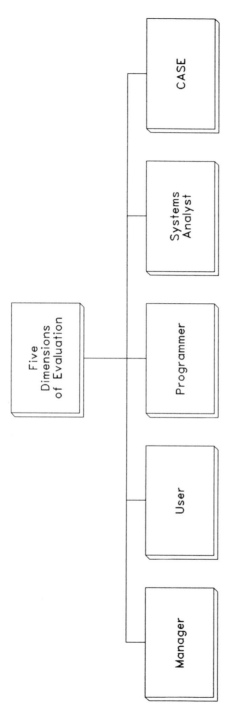

Figure 8.1 Five Dimensions of Analysis

Figure 8.2 Evaluation Approach

8.2 EVALUATING MANAGEMENT COMPONENTS

Figure 8.3 shows the management evaluation criteria used along with the score for HIPO and HIPO-II. Scores are numbers from 1 to 10 with 10 being exceptionally good and 1 being very poor. The values shown for HIPO and HIPO-II are based on the author's experience and should be modified as desired. They are included for illustrative purposes only. In addition, you will want to fill in the values for your favorite design technique. The evaluation criteria have the following meanings:

Manageability—the degree to which the technique supports standard management techniques for project decomposition,

	SADT	JM	WOM	HOS	HIPO	NS	HIPO-II
Manageability					5		10
Cost Estimation					5		10
Scheduling Support					5		10
Risk Management					4		10
Learning Curve					10		9
Life Cycle Range					2		8
Design Complexity.					5		10
Software Capture					5		10
Teamwork					3		9
Configuration Management					3		8
Phase Definition					5		10
Review Capabilities					10		10
Extent of Usage					5		2

Figure 8.3 Management Evaluation Scores

in-process status checking, and control. How well does the tool facilitate communication between the project manager and the systems analyst?

Cost Estimation—the extent to which the technique supports software cost estimation, cost-benefit trade-offs, and design-to-cost efforts

Scheduling Support—the degree to which the technique supports standard scheduling methodologies. Does the technique include provisions for managing resource leveling and resource cohesion? Does the technique support scheduling programs?

Risk Management—the extent to which the technique is compatible with standard management approaches to risk management

Learning Curve—the ease with which a new project team member may learn the design technique and the tools that go with it

Life Cycle Range—the way in which the technique supports all stages of software design: concept oriented, function oriented, and implementation oriented. How easy is the transition from one design stage to another?

Design Complexity—the flexibility of the design technique with designs of varying complexity. Are the designs only as complex as the problem requires? If a large application is conceptually simple, is the design simple?

Software Capture—the extent to which the technique encourages and supports capturing of previous designs, code, etc., for incorporation in a new project

Teamwork—the degree to which the technique supports, rather than hinders, teamwork. Does the technique facilitate independent development of modules with a minimum of coordination?

Configuration Management—the suitability of the technique for tracking and maintaining emerging work products. Does the technique support a method of preventing programmers from coding to old designs (using on-line documentation or other configuration control approaches)?

Phase Definitions—the extent to which the technique highlights project phases that support intermediate deliveries and/or design-to-cost decisions

Review Capabilities—the ease with which the technique may be understood by nontechnical reviewers. Does the technique support reviews at varying levels of detail?

Extent of Usage—the degree to which the technique is used.

Figure 8.4 shows the relative importance of each of these management factors. Notice that these weighting factors add up to 1.0. Figure 8.5 is used to record the weighted scores of each design technique, obtained by multiplying the unweighted score from Fig. 8.3 by the weighting factor in Fig. 8.4. Figure 8.6 is used to summarize the performance of each design technique in the management dimension. The summary values are obtained by adding each column from Fig. 8.5.

	Importance
Manageability	.20
Cost Estimation	.05
Scheduling Support	.05
Risk Management	.05
Learning Curve	.10
Life Cycle Range	.05
Design Complexity	.10
Software Capture	.10
Teamwork	.05
Configuration Management	.05
Phase Definition	.05
Review Capabilities	.10
Extent of Usage	.05

Figure 8.4 Relative Importance of Management Factors

	SADT	JM	WOM	HOS	HIPO	NS	HIPO-II
Manageability					1.0		2.0
Cost Estimation					.2		.5
Scheduling Support					.2		.5
Risk Management					.2		.5
Learning Curve					1.0		.9
Life Cycle Range					.1		.4
Design Complexity					.5		1.0
Software Capture					.5		1.0
Teamwork					.2		.4
Configuration Management					.2		.4
Phase Definition					.2		.5
Review Capabilities					1.0		1.0
Extent of Usage					.2		.1

Figure 8.5   Weighted Management Factor Scores

	Rating
Struct Anal Des Tech (SADT)	
Jackson (JM)	
Warnier-Orr (WOM)	
High Order Soft (HOS)	
HIPO	5.5
Nassi-Shneiderman (NS)	
HIPO-II	9.2

Figure 8.6   Summary of Performance in Management Dimension

8.3 EVALUATING USER-ORIENTED COMPONENTS

For this evaluation dimension, the user is considered to be a nontechnical customer who will be responsible for eventually operating the finished software. This evaluation dimension examines the degree to which the user is involved in the software design process. Figure 8.7 shows the user-oriented evaluation criteria template. The evaluation criteria have the following meanings:

Understandability—the degree to which a nontechnical but otherwise interested user can understand and effectively critique the design outputs

User-Oriented Design—the extent to which the design technique concentrates on user aspects of the software design rather than internal operations of the computer

Prototyping—the extent to which the technique supports prototyping of the user interface

Hand Sketches—if the users reviewing the documents have suggested changes, the ease with which they can sketch the suggested changes directly on the design documents

User Designs—as the users become more familiar with the design technique and software in general, the ease with which the users can begin doing preliminary design of their own software. This preliminary design would then be provided to the systems analyst as a requirements specification and used as a starting point for the detailed design.

Figure 8.8 shows the relative importance of each of these user-oriented factors. Notice that these weighting factors add up to 1.0.

	SADT	JM	WOM	HOS	HIPO	NS	HIPO-II
Understandability					10		9
User Oriented Design					7		9
Prototyping					3		9
Hand Sketches					10		10
User Designs					8		9

Figure 8.7   User-Oriented Evaluation Scores

Figure 8.9 is used to record the weighted scores of each design technique, obtained by multiplying the unweighted score from Fig. 8.7 by the weighting factor in Fig. 8.8. Figure 8.10 is used to summarize the performance of each design technique in the user dimension.

	Importance
Understandability	.30
User Oriented Design	.30
Prototyping	.20 .
Hand Sketches	.10
User Designs	.10

Figure 8.8   Relative Importance of User-Oriented Dimension

	SADT	JM	WOM	HOS	HIPO	NS	HIPO-II
Understandability					3.0		2.7
User Oriented Design					2.1		1.8
Prototyping					.6		1.8
Hand Sketches					1.0		1.0
User Designs					.8		.9

Figure 8.9   Weighted User-Oriented Factor Scores

	Rating
Struct Anal Des Tech (SADT)	
Jackson (JM)	
Warnier-Orr (WOM)	
High Order Soft (HOS)	
HIPO	7.5
Nassi-Shneiderman (NS)	
HIPO-II	8.2

Figure 8.10   Summary of Performance in User-Oriented Dimension

8.4 EVALUATING PROGRAMMER-ORIENTED COMPONENTS

Even the best designs can become terrible programs if the individuals writing the code misinterpret the design or become frustrated and ignore design specifications. A design technique should help the programmers with their work, not present a hurdle to be overcome. Figure 8.11 shows the programmer-oriented evaluation criteria template. The evaluation criteria have the following meanings:

Understandability—the ease with which junior programmers can understand the design documents sufficiently to properly perform their job

Overview Capability—the extent to which the design technique provides the programmer with an overview of the program operation to allow low-level design decisions to be put in perspective

Verification and Validation—the degree to which the technique supports and simplifies the job of module unit testing and program integration testing

Faster Development—the ease with which the design technique allows design products to be used directly during coding without requiring the programmers to start from scratch during coding

Figure 8.12 shows the relative importance of each of these programmer-oriented factors. Figure 8.13 is used to record the weighted scores of each design technique, obtained by multiplying the

	SADT	JM	WOM	HOS	HIPO	NS	HIPO-II
Understandability					3		10
Overview Capability					10		10
Verification & Validation					1		9
Faster Development					1		8

Figure 8.11   Programmer-Oriented Evaluation Scores

unweighted score from Fig. 8.11 by the weighting factor in Fig. 8.12. Figure 8.14 is used to summarize the performance of each design technique in the programmer dimension.

	Importance
Understandability	.30
Overview Capability	.10
Verification & Validation	.30
Faster Development	.30

Figure 8.12   Relative Importance of Programmer-Oriented Factors

	SADT	JM	WOM	HOS	HIPO	NS	HIPO-II
Understandability					.9		3.0
Overview Capability					1.0		1.0
Verification & Validation					.3		2.7
Faster Development					.3		2.4

Figure 8.13   Weighted Programmer-Oriented Factor Scores

	Rating
Struct Anal Des Tech (SADT)	
Jackson (JM)	
Warnier-Orr (WOM)	
High Order Soft (HOS)	
HIPO	2.5
Nassi-Shneiderman (NS)	
HIPO-II	9.1

Figure 8.14   Summary of Performance in Programmer-Oriented Dimension

8.5 EVALUATING SYSTEMS ANALYST-ORIENTED COMPONENTS

The person most affected by the choice of a design technique is the systems analyst. The systems analyst must work with the tool day in and day out. The systems analyst is less concerned with the time needed to learn the technique, and more concerned with the capabilities available after an appropriate learning period. Ease of use is critical. Figure 8.15 shows the systems analyst-oriented evaluation criteria template. The evaluation criteria have the following meanings:

Problem Decomposition—the ease with which a problem can be represented by components that are suitable for software implementation. Hierarchical decompositions are preferred.

Stepwise Refinement—the effectiveness of the technique in the stepwise refinement of the problem to ever-increasing levels of detail

Functional Analysis—the degree to which the technique supports effective functional decomposition of the problem. Does the technique recognize that all functional elements are not identical? Does the technique handle modeling of user interaction, interrupt handling, and common functions?

Data Analysis—the degree to which the technique supports analysis and design of the data aspects of the program. Does the technique support a global data hierarchy? Does the technique support data flow analysis?

Algorithm Analysis—the extent to which the technique supports design and representation of the program algorithms. Are the five basic control flow constructs (sequence, iteration, alternation, recursion, and concurrency) supported? Is the algorithm representation sufficiently detailed to allow the programmers to implement the module without further guidance?

Black Box Interfaces—the extent to which the boundaries between modules are distinct and well defined. Are modules defined primarily in terms of their inputs and outputs?

Quick to Generate—the ease with which one can quickly document a design in a format suitable for review and use by the program implementors

	SADT	JM	WOM	HOS	HIPO	NS	HIPO-II
Problem Decomposition					4		10
Stepwise Refinement					7		10
Functional Analysis					5		10
Data Analysis					1		8
Algorithm Analysis					6		9
Black Box Interface					8		9
Quick to Generate					9		8
Quick to Change					5		10
Validation					1		6
Suitability - Embedded Sys					3		8
Suitability - Scientific					2		9
Suitability - Op. Systems					4		7
Suitability - Utilities					4		8
Suitability - Business					5		7
Suitability - AI					2		7
Suitability - Small					6		10
Suitability - Medium					5		10
Suitability - Large					4		10

Figure 8.15   Systems Analyst Evaluation Scores

Quick to Change—the ease with which one can modify the design during the life of the project

Validation—the extent to which automatic verification of the design is supported

Suitability–Embedded Systems—the degree to which the technique is appropriate for use when developing embedded systems

Suitability–Scientific/Engineering—the degree to which the technique is appropriate for use when developing scientific/engineering applications

Suitability–Operating Systems—the degree to which the technique is appropriate for use when developing operating systems

Suitability–Utilities—the degree to which the technique is appropriate for use when developing utilities

Suitability–Business—the degree to which the technique is appropriate for use when developing business applications

Suitability–Artificial Intelligence—the degree to which the technique is appropriate for use when developing artificial intelligence applications

Suitability–Small Systems—the degree to which the technique is appropriate for use when developing small systems (less than $200,000)

	Importance
Problem Decomposition	.10
Stepwise Refinement	.05
Functional Analysis	.05
Data Analysis	.05
Algorithm Analysis	.05
Black Box Interfaces	.05
Quick to Generate	.05
Quick to Change	.10
Validation	.05
Suitability - Embedded Sys	.05
Suitability - Scientific	.05
Suitability - Op. Sys.	.05
Suitability - Utilities	.05
Suitability - Business	.05
Suitability - AI	.05
Suitability - Small	.05
Suitability - Medium	.05
Suitability - Large	.05

Figure 8.16   Relative Importance of Systems Analyst Factors

Suitability–Medium Systems—the degree to which the technique
is appropriate for use when developing medium-sized systems ($200,000–$3,000,000)

Suitability–Large Systems—the degree to which the technique is
appropriate for use when developing large-sized systems
(over $3,000,000)

Figure 8.16 shows the relative importance of each of these
systems analyst-oriented factors. Figure 8.17 is used to record the
weighted scores of each design technique, obtained by multiplying the
unweighted score from Fig. 8.15 by the weighting factor in Fig. 8.16.
Figure 8.18 is used to summarize the performance of each design
technique in the systems analyst dimension.

	SADT	JM	WOM	HOS	HIPO	NS	HIPO-II
Problem Decomposition					.4		1.0
Stepwise Refinement					.4		.5
Functional Analysis					.2		.5
Data Analysis					.0		.4
Algorithm Analysis					.3		.4
Black Box Interface					.4		.4
Quick to Generate					.4		.4
Quick to Change					.5		1.0
Validation					.0		.3
Suitability - Embedded Sys					.2		.4
Suitability - Scientific					.1		.4
Suitability - Op. Systems					.2		.4
Suitability - Utilities					.2		.4
Suitability - Business					.2		.4
Suitability - AI					.1		.4
Suitability - Small					.3		.5
Suitability - Medium					.2		.5
Suitability - Large					.2		.5

Figure 8.17 Weighted Systems Analyst Factor Scores

	Rating
Struct Anal Des Tech (SADT)	
Jackson (JM)	
Warnier-Orr (WOM)	
High Order Soft (HOS)	
HIPO	4.3
Nassi-Shneiderman (NS)	
HIPO-II	8.8

Figure 8.18   Summary of Performance in Systems Analyst Dimension

8.6 EVALUATING COMPUTER-AIDED SOFTWARE ENGINEERING (CASE) COMPONENTS

Although it is possible to automate any of the design techniques, some are significantly more suited for computer automation than others. Design techniques that require graphic terminals are more expensive in terms of computer hardware and performance. Techniques that require plotters for producing the outputs are slow and require hardware most users do not already have. Figure 8.19 shows the CASE-oriented evaluation criteria template. The evaluation criteria have the following meanings:

> *Computer Support*—the availability of low-cost (less than $1,000) software to implement all aspects of the design approach. Does the software run on a low-cost personal computer?

	SADT	JM	WOM	HOS	HIPO	NS	HIPO-II
Computer Support					1		10
System Editing					10		10
Printer Support					5		10
Support					2		1
Features					1		10

Figure 8.19   CASE-Oriented Evaluation Scores

Screen Editing—the suitability of the technique for editing directly on a computer screen. Can the design be represented without requiring graphics capability (which is slow)? How compact is the design, that is, how much of the design can fit on a standard terminal?

Printer Support—the feasibility of printing the design outputs on a standard dot matrix or laser printer. Once again, techniques requiring that the outputs be printed in a printer's graphics mode are penalized because graphic output is significantly slower than text output.

Support—the degree to which the available software is supported in terms of classes, training, and technical support

Features—the extent of the design and editing features (windowing, variable levels of detail, flexible formats, etc.) built into the CASE systems available

Figure 8.20 shows the relative importance of each of these CASE-oriented factors. Figure 8.21 is used to record the weighted scores of each design technique, obtained by multiplying the un-

	Importance
Computer Support	.20
Screen Editing	.20
Printer Support	.20
Support	.20
Features	.20

Figure 8.20   Relative Importance of CASE-Oriented Factors

	SADT	JM	WOM	HOS	HIPO	NS	HIPO-II
Computer Support					.2		2.0
System Editing					2.0		2.0
Printer Support					1.0		2.0
Support					.4		.2
Features					.2		2.0

Figure 8.21   Weighted CASE-Oriented Factor Scores

	Rating
Struct Anal Des Tech (SADT)	
Jackson (JM)	
Warnier-Orr (WOM)	
High Order Soft (HOS)	
HIPO	3.8
Nassi-Shneiderman (NS)	
HIPO-II	8.2

Figure 8.22   Summary of Performance in CASE-Oriented Factors

weighted score from Fig. 8.19 by the weighting factor in Fig. 8.20. Figure 8.22 is used to summarize the performance of each design technique in the CASE dimension.

8.7 SUMMARY EVALUATION

Figure 8.23 shows the weighting factor for each of the five dimensions of our evaluation. Figure 8.24 is used to record the weighted scores of each design technique, obtained by multiplying the summary scores from Figs. 8.6, 8.10, 8.14, 8.18, and 8.21 by the weighting factors shown in Fig. 8.22. Figure 8.25 is used to summarize the performance of each design technique across all evaluation dimensions.

	Importance
Management Components	.30
User Oriented Components	.20
Programmer Components	.10
Systems Analyst Components	.30
CASE Components	.10

Figure 8.23   Relative Importance of Each Dimension of Evaluation

	SADT	JM	WOM	HOS	HIPO	NS	HIPO-II
Management					1.6		2.8
User					1.5		1.6
Programmer					0.2		0.9
Systems Analyst					1.3		2.6
CASE					0.4		0.8

Figure 8.24   Summary Evaluation Scores

	Rating
Struct Anal Des Tech (SADT)	
Jackson (JM)	
Warnier-Orr (WOM)	
High Order Soft (HOS)	
HIPO	5.0
Nassi-Shneiderman (NS)	
HIPO-II	8.7

Figure 8.25   Summary Rating

chapter
9

STRUCTURED DESIGNER'S TOOLBOX

Although it is certainly possible to design software without the assistance of a computer, a computer can drastically improve both your efficiency and effectiveness. Using a computer, software design is faster and simpler. Revisions to the design are easy, allowing you to perform effective "what if" analysis and to maintain an accurate design in an environment of changing requirements. In addition, the computer allows you to model the program's user interface early in the design process. One of the significant advantages of HIPO-II is that the design representations used by HIPO-II were chosen to be compatible with low-cost Computer-Aided Software Engineering (CASE) capabilities.

The author has developed a computer program that implements the theories described in this book. *Structured Designer's Toolbox* (SDT) runs on an IBM-PC and prints all outputs using a low-cost dot matrix or laser printer. The program directly interfaces with the computer program *Structured Project Manager's Toolbox*[1] (also by the author) to allow the systems analyst and project manager to closely coordinate their efforts. Because SDT is typical of CASE tools that will support HIPO-II, this program will be discussed in detail in this chapter.

The SDT top menu contains the following choices:

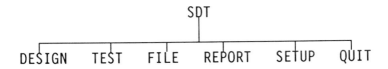

Design

The design option is used to generate the program data hierarchy, functional hierarchy, control flow, input-output (header) definitions, pseudocode, and sample outputs.

Test

This option validates the data flows for consistency and "runs" the program. The Test option is used by the systems analyst to check work to date, and by the customer to review the design. Running the program consists of SDT generating a prototype of the user interface, including

- All menu displays
- All interrupt- and keyboard-activated processing
- Displays of screens, overlays, data entry forms, and reports as defined during the design process

This option also can be used to validate/debug the program's control flow by allowing the analyst to single-step through the program's calling sequence while examining variables and/or pseudo-coded algorithms.

---

[1]Structured Project Manager's Toolbox is a project management program which is also available from the author.

File

This option allows the design to be saved and retrieved to and from disk. The File option also allows electronic downloading of design information to *Structured Project Manager's Toolbox.*

Report

This option prints the design outputs in hard copy format using a standard printer. Reports can also be sent to the screen for review at a terminal, or to disk. Module header definitions and pseudocode are often printed to disk for use by the programming team during implementation. The following reports are available:

- Data hierarchy summaries
- Program hierarchy summary, including control flow (Hierarchy)
- Module Input-Process-Output (IPO) reports in traditional HIPO format
- Module header definitions and pseudocode
- Output screens, overlays, and reports

Setup

This option is used to initialize system variables, modify the display colors, and duplicate the program disk.

Following the HIPO-II design philosophy, SDT supports program design in the following areas:

1. Data design
2. Functional design
3. Data flow design
4. Algorithm design
5. User interface design

In the remainder of this chapter, we will briefly discuss each of these areas. We will also describe some features of SDT designed to facilitate entering and maintaining your program design.

9.1 DATA DESIGN USING SDT

As shown in Fig. 9.1, SDT displays the data hierarchy graphically in a tabular format. The data hierarchy represents on-line and off-line global data bases and variables that are available to all program modules. Column headers have the following meanings:

#—sequential data element number

T—data element type. Valid types are File (F), Record (R), Structure (S), Bit (B), Character (C), Unsigned Character (UC), Integer (I), Unsigned Integer (UI), Long integer (L), Unsigned Long integer (UL), Floating point number (F), Double precision floating point number (D), Other (O).

Name—the name of the data element or variable

Size—if the data element is an array, the value of size tells the dimension of the array. Elements that are not arrays will have a size of one.

Quantity—for data elements representing aggregates of data (file, record, structure), the entry for quantity is the estimated number of elements. Quantity also may be used to represent the second dimension for matrices.

The user's location in the hierarchy is shown via an inverse video cursor. The cursor can be moved through the entire data hierarchy using the up and down arrow keys, page up and down, and home or

```
Add  Modify  Delete  Window  Goto  Quit

Add new data element.
```

#	T	NAME	SIZE	QTY
0	DF	Sample	1	1
1	C	─Name	30	1
2	F	─Latitude	1	1
3	F	─Longitude	1	1
4	I	─Course	1	1
5	I	─Speed	1	1
6	I	└Altitude	1	1

Figure 9.1 Sample Data Structure Representation

end. The Goto option can be used to move the cursor directly to a desired module.

Data elements are added using the Add menu option, resulting in the screen shown in Fig. 9.2. The field for Description is used to enter a brief description of the data, which may include the range and accuracy information.

The data hierarchical structure is intuitively clear, and maintenance of the data hierarchy is quite painless. During implementation, the data hierarchy can be converted quickly to appropriate data definitions in a project header (include) file or disk-based data base. SDT automatically verifies that input and output data referenced in each program module are either explicitly passed or are available in the data hierarchy.

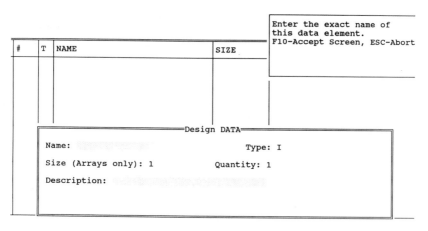

Figure 9.2   Sample CASE Add Data Form

9.2 PROGRAM HIERARCHY DESIGN USING SDT

SDT supports all six module classes defined by HIPO-II (Menu, Key, Interrupt, Processing, Common, and Library). As with the data hierarchy, SDT displays the program hierarchy in a tabular fashion (see Fig. 9.3). The column headers have the following meanings:

#—sequential module number

T—module type. Valid types are Menu (M), Key (K), Interrupt (I), Processing (P), Common (C), and Library (L).

```
Add  Modify  Specify  Header  Process  Delete  Range  View  Goto  Quit

Add new program element.
```

#	T	NAME	SCREEN	S TYPE	HEADER	P CODE
0	P	Project Alpha		N	N	N
1	M	─Design		N	N	N
2	M	├─Data		N	N	N
3	M	└─Program		N	N	N
4	M	─Test		N	N	N
5	M	─File		N	N	N
6	M	─Report		N	N	N
7	M	├─Report 1		N	N	N
8	M	└─Report 2		N	N	N
9	M	└─Setup		N	N	N

```
Maximum tasks: 1500                                        View: 99
```

Figure 9.3   Sample SDT Program Hierarchy Screen

Name—module name

Screen—sample screen number. Used when copying or moving screen definitions between modules.

S Type—sample screen type. Valid types are None (N), Screen (S), Overlay (O), and Report (R).

Header—indicates if the module header information (Input-Output) has been entered (Y) or not (N)

P Code—indicates if the module pseudocode has been entered (Y) or not (N)

The Add option is used to add modules to the hierarchy under the current cursor location. As each module is added to the program hierarchy, the systems analyst specifies the type of module and the desired level of indentation. SDT then displays a data entry form, as illustrated in Fig. 9.4. The displayed fields have the following meanings:

Name—the name of the module

Description—a brief description of the module function. This information will automatically be included in the module header. For Menu modules, this line is also used as the menu prompt line displayed during prototyping.

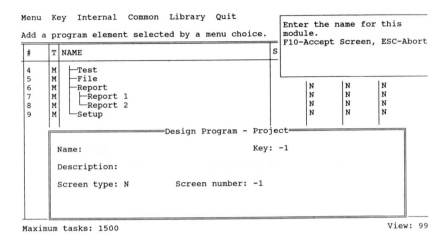

Figure 9.4   Sample Program Module Data Entry Form

Screen Type—tells SDT if this module has a sample screen, overlay, or report associated with it. Overlays are used both for prompt windows and for data entry overlays.

Screen Number—if the module has a sample output associated with it, SDT automatically assigns a unique screen number to the output and displays this number here

As with the data hierarchy, the SDT representation of the program hierarchy is intuitively clear, and on-line editing makes maintenance of the design simple. As you would expect, hierarchical elements can be easily inserted, copied, deleted, and moved. Various versions of the program design can be saved to disk, and portions of the design can be saved to disk to generate a library of design components for use by other projects.

9.3 DATA FLOW DESIGN USING SDT

From the screen showing the program hierarchy, the systems analyst can select a module of interest using the cursor. The menu option Header is then selected to display the form shown in Fig. 9.5. This form defines the module data flow in terms of input and output variables. The meaning for each specific field is described in detail in

Chapter 4. Figure 9.6 shows the same form with typical entries already made. As module headers are defined, the program hierarchy column labeled HEADER will display a Y, allowing quick progress checks of the design effort.

```
Name: Update Posit                         Update coding history with
Desc: Update position of track             name and date of update.
*** Module Coding History ***              F10-Accept Screen, ESC-Abort
1)
2)
3)
4)
Usage:
****************************INPUT PARAMETERS****************************




****************************OUTPUT PARAMETERS***************************



****************************DESCRIPTION********************************



RETURN:
```

Figure 9.5   Sample SDT Input-Process Data Entry Screen

```
Name: Update Posit                         Describe the return value,
Desc: Update position of track             if appropriate.
*** Module Coding History ***              F10-Accept Screen, ESC-Abort
1) WHR 1/1/89 - original design
2) SSD 2/1/89 - added color
3)
4)
Usage: int update_posit(int track_id, int time_duration);
****************************INPUT PARAMETERS****************************
int track_id;                       int speed;
int time_duration;  --in minutes
float lat;  --from file
float long;
int course;
****************************OUTPUT PARAMETERS***************************
float lat; --to file
float long;
int retval;
****************************DESCRIPTION********************************
Module updates unit's position in file using current course and
speed.  PIM leg duration is set by time_duration.  New positions are
calculated using Rhumb line calculations.
RETURN: int retval; 0 = success, -1 for error
```

Figure 9.6   Completed SDT Header Definition Form

9.4 ALGORITHM DESIGN USING SDT

The procedure for entering the module pseudocode is identical to that
for entering the module header information. The module of interest is
selected using the cursor, and the menu option Process is selected.
Figure 9.7 shows a partially completed pseudocode definition form.
After a module's pseudocode is defined, the program hierarchy column
labeled P CODE will display a Y, allowing quick progress checks of
the design effort.

In addition to standard pseudocode, SDT allows truth tables,
brief textual descriptions, and resource limitations (memory, CPU
cycles, etc.) to be included on this form. Editing features for inserting
and deleting lines are supported.

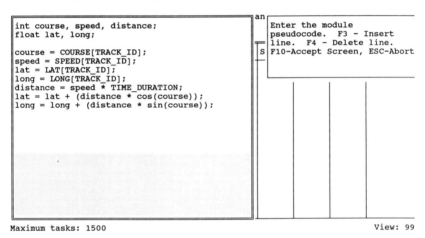

```
int course, speed, distance;
float lat, long;

course = COURSE[TRACK_ID];
speed = SPEED[TRACK_ID];
lat = LAT[TRACK_ID];
long = LONG[TRACK_ID];
distance = speed * TIME_DURATION;
lat = lat + (distance * cos(course));
long = long + (distance * sin(course));
```

```
Enter the module
pseudocode.  F3 - Insert
line.  F4 - Delete line.
F10-Accept Screen, ESC-Abort
```

Maximum tasks: 1500   View: 99

Figure 9.7   Sample SDT Pseudocode Form

9.5 USER INTERFACE DESIGN USING SDT

As the program hierarchy is developed, the designer determines which
modules should include a sample screen, report, or overlay. When the
SDT-generated prototype is run, SDT will display sample outputs in
the output area of Fig. 9.8. These sample outputs are typically defined
for the following three module types:

   1. **Menu Modules:** Menu modules that are at the bottom of the
      menu hierarchy will often have a sample screen or report

```
┌─────────────────────────────────────────────────────────────┐
│ Menu choices line 1.                                          │
│ Menu choices line 2.                                          │
│ Menu specific prompt line.                                    │
│═════════════════════════════════════════════════════════════│
│                                                               │
│                                                               │
│              Output Screens                                   │
│                      Reports                                  │
│                              Overlays                         │
│                                                               │
│                                                               │
│                                                               │
│                                                               │
│                                                               │
└─────────────────────────────────────────────────────────────┘
```

Figure 9.8   HIPO-II CASE Prototype Screen Layout

associated with them. Some menu options will use a sample overlay either to display a message indicating some processing that will occur or to display a sample data entry form.

2. **Key Modules:** During a program test (prototyping), key modules are activated by the user pressing the appropriate key. These modules will then normally display a new overlay or screen. For example, to demonstrate the Up Arrow key processing for an application, you might display a sample screen, then have the key module associated with Up Arrow display the same screen with the cursor moved one line up. This could be accomplished by copying the sample screen to the key module, then moving the location of the highlighted cursor.

3. **Interrupt Modules:** Although interrupt modules often are activated by an external interrupt, SDT allows the interrupt to be simulated by a key press when testing the program. Overlays are often attached to interrupt modules to display a message confirming what action is being taken.

SDT allows output definitions to be copied between modules, deleted, and modified. Output definitions can also be written to and read from disk to allow output design libraries to be built up. Outputs can consist of any character from the IBM ASCII and extended character set, including line drawing characters. Screens can have any mixture of display attributes (colors, reverse video, blinking, etc.). Overlays can be positioned anywhere in the output area, and can be any size.

9.6 SDT EDITING FEATURES

To facilitate entering and maintaining the program design, SDT includes some advanced editing features, including

- Variable views
- Windows
- Range operations

Variable Views

During design reviews, it is often true that too much information can be more confusing than too little. SDT allows the design to be reviewed at varying levels of detail. Program hierarchy elements that have additional detail not shown on the screen are displayed in brackets[]. Figure 9.9 shows a sample program hierarchy with hidden detail. The displayed view (amount of detail) can be modified using any combination of the following two approaches:

1. **Modify the View:** The program view is defined as the lowest level of the hierarchy that will be displayed. The top of the hierarchy is level 0, the next level of detail is level 1, the next

```
Increase  Decrease  Expand  Contract  All  Window  Quit

Increase current view.
```

#	T	NAME	SCREEN	S TYPE	HEADER	P CODE
0	P	Project Alpha		N	N	N
1	M	─Menu choice 1		N	N	N
2	M	├─[Choice 1.a]		N	N	N
4	M	├─[Choice 1.b]		N	N	N
6	M	└─[Choice 1.c]		N	N	N
8	M	─Menu Choice 2		N	N	N
9	M	─Menu Choice 3		N	N	N
10	M	└─Menu Choice 4		N	N	N

```
Maximum tasks: 1500                                    View: 99
```

Figure 9.9 Program Hierarchy with Hidden Detail

level of detail is level 2, etc. If the view is set to level 4, only the first five (0–4) levels of the hierarchy will be displayed. The view can be increased or decreased with a single key press. This option is useful when describing or reviewing top-level decompositions of the program. Figure 9.10 illustrates this concept.

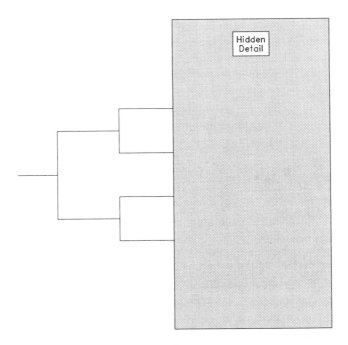

Figure 9.10   Hierarchical View

2. **Expand or Contract Tasks:** While modifying the view affects the entire program hierarchy, expand and contract affect only a single task. Contract can be used to hide all detailed processing for any selected task. This is especially useful when a task's complete description is not ready for review. Expand is used to selectively display additional detail for a given task. Expand is useful if the reviewer requires additional details about a module to complete the review. Figure 9.11 illustrates this concept.

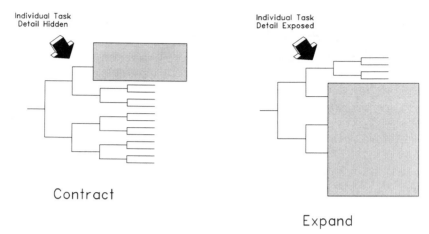

Figure 9.11   Expand or Contract Task

In addition, the systems analyst can set the view to All to display the entire program hierarchy with no hidden detail.

Windows

When designing a program, it is often useful to simultaneously view one portion of the program hierarchy while working on another. This might be useful when ensuring interface compatibility, duplicating a design approach, or copying sections of the design from one location to another. SDT supports these operations by allowing the program hierarchy to be windowed (see Fig. 9.12). The cursor can be moved back and forth between the windows when copying or reviewing sections of the program.

Range Operations

SDT allows many operations to be performed on a user-designated range of program hierarchy elements. These operations include

Move—move the flagged tasks to a new location

Copy—copy the flagged tasks to a new location

Extract—write the flagged tasks to a disk file. Useful when generating libraries of program design elements for use on other programs.

```
Increase  Decrease  Expand  Contract  All  Window  Quit

Increase current view.
```

#	T	NAME	SCREEN	S TYPE	HEADER	P CODE
1	M	├─Menu choice 1		N	N	N
2	M	│ ├─Choice 1.a		N	N	N
3	M	│ │ ├─a		N	N	N
4	M	│ │ ├─b		N	N	N
5	M	│ │ └─c		N	N	N
6	M	│ ├─[Choice 1.b]		N	N	N
8	M	│ └─[Choice 1.c]		N	N	N
10	M	├─Menu Choice 2		N	N	N
0	P	Project Alpha		N	N	N
1	M	├─Menu choice 1		N	N	N
2	M	│ ├─[Choice 1.a]		N	N	N
10	M	│ ├─[Choice 1.b]		N	N	N
12	M	│ └─[Choice 1.c]		N	N	N
14	M	├─Menu Choice 2		N	N	N
15	M	├─Menu Choice 3		N	N	N
16	M	└─Menu Choice 4		N	N	N

```
Maximum tasks: 1500                                          View: 99
```

Figure 9.12   Sample SDT Windowed Hierarchy

Insert—insert tasks from a disk file at the current cursor location

Shift—shift the flagged tasks to a new level in the hierarchy. Used when inserting or deleting levels from the program hierarchy.

9.7 ORDERING SDT

Structured Designer's Toolbox (SDT) can be ordered for $492 plus $6 for shipping and handling (plus sales tax for California residents). Shipments are normally made via UPS (prepaid or COD). UPS second-day air shipments are available for an additional $3 shipping charge. International shipments must be prepaid in U.S. funds, and the international shipping charges are $12.

To order a copy of SDT, please contact:

William H. Roetzheim & Associates

3891 American Avenue

La Mesa, CA 92041

(619) 464-0182

NOTE: This book includes a form that may be used to order a copy of SDT.

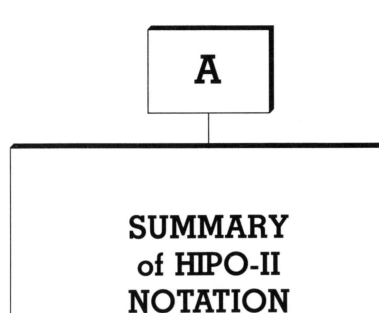

A

SUMMARY of HIPO-II NOTATION

This appendix presents a brief summary of HIPO-II notation. Hierarchical notation is shown in the format that would be used if the design was prepared manually without using the CASE features of *Structured Designer's Toolbox*.

A.1 DATA HIERARCHY

General Structure

Data structures are represented hierarchically.

```
Sample Data
  ├─Track File
  │   └─Track Record
  │        ├─Item 1
  │        ├─Item 2
  │        └─Item 3
  ├─Element 2
  └─Element 3
```

Data Types

Data types are written in parentheses next to each data element. Some typical types are File (F), Record (R), Structure (S), Bit (B), Character (C), Unsigned Character (UC), Integer (I), Unsigned Integer (UI), Long integer (L), Unsigned Long integer (UL), Floating point number (F), Double precision floating point number (D).

```
Sample Data
 ├─Track File (DF)
 │  └─Track Record (R)
 │     ├─Item 1 (C)
 │     ├─Item 2 (I)
 │     └─Item 3 (F)
 ├─Element 2 (S)
 └─Element 3 (C)
```

Arrays.   If the data element is actually an array of the appropriate type, the size of the array is shown next to the data element.

```
Sample Data
 ├─Track File (DF)
 │  └─Track Record (R)
 │     ├─Item 1 (C) [30]
 │     ├─Item 2 (I)
 │     └─Item 3 (F) [10]
 ├─Element 2 (S)
 └─Element 3 (C)
```

Quantity.   For data elements representing aggregates of data (file, record, structure), the estimated quantity of aggregate elements is shown next to the data element. Whether the number represents an array size or aggregate quantity is based on the data element type.

```
Sample Data
 ├─Track File (DF)
 │  └─Track Record (R) [1000]
 │     ├─Item 1 (C) [30]
 │     ├─Item 2 (I)
 │     └─Item 3 (F) [10]
 ├─Element 2 (S) [100]
 └─Element 3 (C)
```

Matrices.   Matrices are represented by showing both matrix dimensions separated by a comma.

```
Sample Data
  ├─Track File (DF)
  │   └─Track Record (R) [1000]
  │       ├─Item 1 (C) [30]
  │       ├─Item 2 (I)
  │       └─Item 3 (F) [10,10]
  ├─Element 2 (S) [100]
  └─Element 3 (C)
```

A.2 PROGRAM HIERARCHY

General Structure

Program structures are represented hierarchically.

```
Project Alpha
  ├─Design
  │   ├─Data
  │   └─Program
  │       ├─Add_Task
  │       └─Delete_Task
  ├─Test
  ├─Report
  │   ├─Report_1
  │   └─Report_2
  ├─File
  └─Setup
```

Module Types

Module types are written in parentheses next to each program module. Some typical types are Menu choice (M), Interrupt (I), Key-activated (K), Processing (P), Common (C), and Library (L). The concept- and function-oriented design normally will contain only Menu, Interrupt, and Key modules. The implementation-oriented design will add the Processing, Common, and Library modules.

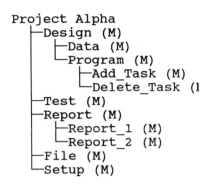

```
Project Alpha
  ├─Design (M)
  │   ├─Data (M)
  │   └─Program (M)
  │       ├─Add_Task (M)
  │       └─Delete_Task (1
  ├─Test (M)
  ├─Report (M)
  │   ├─Report_1 (M)
  │   └─Report_2 (M)
  ├─File (M)
  └─Setup (M)
```

Sequence.   Sequential control flow is shown by a single line (the default). Program logic executes from top to bottom of the program hierarchy.

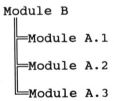

```
Module A
  │
  ├─Module A.1
  │
  ├─Module A.2
  │
  └─Module A.3
```

Iteration.   Program loops are shown using a double line.

```
Module B
  ║
  ╠═Module A.1
  ║
  ╠═Module A.2
  ║
  ╚═Module A.3
```

Alternation.   Conditional execution is shown using a brace to connect the program module to the hierarchy.

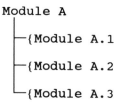

```
Module A

 ─{Module A.1

 ─{Module A.2

 ─{Module A.3
```

Concurrency.   Concurrent execution is shown using an epsilon to connect the program module to the hierarchy. Note that a module may be both conditional and concurrent.

```
Module A

 ─εModule A.1

 ─εModule A.2

 ─εModule A.3
```

Recursion.   Recursion is shown by putting a module under itself. The lower level copy of the module is of type Common.

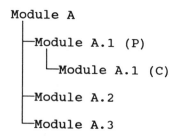

```
Module A

 ─Module A.1 (P)

    └Module A.1 (C)

 ─Module A.2

 ─Module A.3
```

Input-Process-Output

Module detailed descriptions involve completing the form shown in Fig. A.1. Chapter 4 describes each field in depth. The USAGE field contains an example of how the module is called. INPUT and OUTPUT parameters include both global data and those explicitly

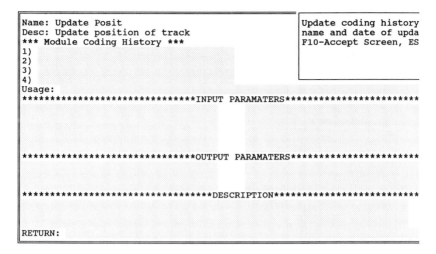

Figure A.1   Sample HIPO-II Input-Process Data Entry Screen

passed, and are shown in all upper case. PSEUDOCODE uses a freeform structured english to describe the module algorithm, with the pseudocode syntax chosen to be similar to the language used for implementation.

As the module descriptions are completed, a Y is written next to the module name on the program hierarchy.

```
Project Alpha
     ├─Design (M) -Y-
     │    ├─Data (M)    -Y-  [1-Screen]
     │    └─Program (M) -Y-  [2-Screen]
     │         ├─Add_Task (M) -Y-   [3-Overlay]
     │         └─Delete_Task (M) -Y-   [4-Overlay]
     ├─Test (M) -Y-
     ├─Report (M)
     │    ├─Report_1 (M) [5-Report]
     │    └─Report_2 (M) [6-Report]
     ├─File (M)
     └─Setup (M) -Y-
```

A *Y* Shows the Module Description is Complete

Sample Outputs

Menu, Key, and Interrupt modules may have sample outputs included in the design. Sample outputs may be screens, reports, or overlays. Overlays are a window that is output on top of the current screen. If a program module has a sample output defined, the output number is written next to the module on the program hierarchy. The output number is then used to reference a document containing all output definitions.

```
Project Alpha
   ├─Design (M)
   │    ├─Data (M)     [1-Screen]
   │    └─Program (M) [2-Screen]
   │         ├─Add_Task (M) [3-Overlay]
   │         └─Delete_Task (M) [4-Overlay]
   ├─Test (M)
   ├─Report (M)
   │    ├─Report_1 (M) [5-Report]
   │    └─Report_2 (M) [6-Report]
   ├─File (M)
   └─Setup (M)
```

Sample Outputs Associated with Menu, Keyboard, and Interrupt Modules

B

USING HIPO-II
on
MILITARY PROJECTS

The largest customer for software development in the world is the U. S. government, and within the government, the military. Developing software for the military can be extremely profitable, fun, and relatively risk-free—if you know the ropes. If you are not currently involved in work for this market segment (or you would like to expand your military software opportunities), simply follow the guidelines in my book *Proposal Writing for the Data Processing Consultant* (Prentice-Hall, 1986). This book clarifies the process the government uses to procure software, and presents step-by-step plans for marketing your skills to the government.

Even if you do not anticipate entering the military software development arena, knowledge of military software development practices and procedures can benefit you. Military contractors are routinely required to produce huge programs to rigid requirements, and the programs must operate without serious flaw. This is accomplished using a rigidly structured development procedure that ensures consistent quality, although at an increased cost. Many of these techniques can be relaxed somewhat and applied to development of large commercial systems.

In the remainder of this appendix, we will cover the following:

- Military documents applicable to software development
- Military system hierarchies and decompositions
- Military software development life cycle
- Military software development dependencies
- Military software documentation requirements

Most of the background material in this chapter comes from Appendix A of my book *Structured Computer Project Management*. If you have recently read this book, or are very familiar with military software development, you might want to skip to the following sections of this appendix:

- Section B.4, Military Software Development Life Cycle, describes how the various components of structured software development and stages of software design (as identified in this book) fit into the military software development life cycle
- Section B.5, Military Software Documentation Requirements, has been greatly expanded to describe how HIPO-II design documents fit into required Data Item Deliverables (DIDs).

You might also notice some minor changes in the software DIDs and project decomposition. These changes are necessary to reflect the latest version of DOD-STD-2167 (released in mid–1988). The new version is DOD-STD-2167A.

B.1 MILITARY STANDARDS APPLICABLE TO SOFTWARE DEVELOPMENT

You can't play the game unless you know the rules, and the rulebooks for military software development are called military standards and specifications. As shown in Fig. B.1, the primary documents you will want to read (in order of priority) are as follows:

- Department of Defense Standard 2167A (DOD-STD-2167A)
- Department of Defense Handbook 287 (DOD-HDBK-287)

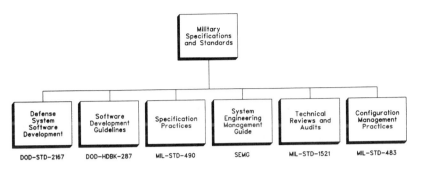

Figure B.1   Military Standards and Specifications

- Military Standard 490A (MIL-STD-490A)
- *System Engineering Management Guide* (SEMG)
- Military Standard 1521B (MIL-STD-1521B)
- Military Standard 483 (MIL-STD-483A)

All of these documents except the SEMG can be ordered from the U.S. Government Printing Office for a nominal fee. The *System Engineering Management Guide* can be obtained from the Defense Systems Management College, Fort Belvoir, VA 22060.

DOD-STD-2167A.   DOD-STD-2167A (Defense System Software Development) is the primary document used to manage military software development. This document ties all other standards together, and describes how generic military requirements are tailored to the software world. In addition, the latest version of this standard (DOD-STD-2167A) includes 17 Data Item Descriptions (DIDs) that describe each document produced during a large development effort (see Fig. B.2).

DOD-HDBK-287.   Although DOD-HDBK-287 (Software Development guidelines) is not invoked as a contractual requirement on software projects, this official guide amplifies and clarifies many of the requirements contained in other military standards. DOD-HDBK-287 also includes algorithms for determining which of the 17 DIDs described in MIL-STD-2167A apply to a specific project. These algorithms are beneficial both to government employees writing contracts and to software developers trying to justify reductions in software documentation requirements.

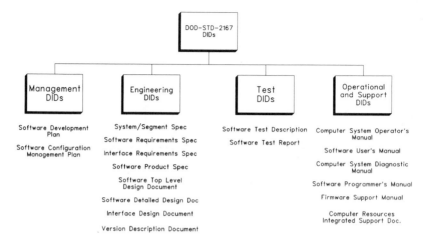

Figure B.2   DOD-STD-2167 Required Documents

MIL-STD-490A.   MIL-STD-490A (Specification Practices) is the primary document used to guide military hardware and system procurements. Because of this, any software project that is part of a larger system will likely be required to follow MIL-STD-490 guidelines. The primary impacts of MIL-STD-490A on you as a software developer are as follows:

- You will receive a type *A* System/Segment Specification, which describes the top-level requirements of the system, some of which must be met by software.
- You will be required to produce a type *B5* Software Development Specification, which is a combination of two documents already required by DOD-STD-2167A (the Software Requirements Specification and Interface Requirements Specification, described later).
- You will be required to produce a type *C5* Software Product Specification, which is a combination of two documents already required by DOD-STD-2167A (the Interface Design Document and Software Design Document, described later), along with the program's source and object code listings.

Figure B.3 summarizes the systemwide deliverables specified in MIL-STD-490A.

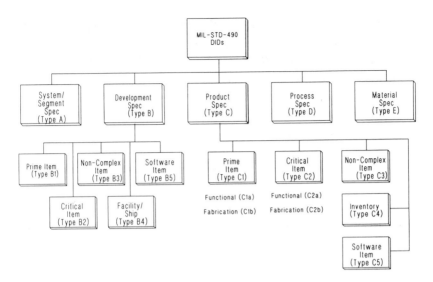

Figure B.3   MIL-STD-490 Required Deliverables

System Engineering Management Guide (SEMG).   The
System Engineering Management Guide has no official status, but is
important to you because most program managers for large military
software development projects follow this manual when managing
their projects. The SEMG covers general system engineering management, system definition tasks, configuration definition and management during the project, technical performance achievement, and
operational feasibility analysis.

MIL-STD-1521B.   MIL-STD-1521B (Technical Reviews and
Audits for Systems, Equipments, and Computer Software) describes
procedures for conducting the following program reviews:

- System Requirements Review
- System Design Review
- Software Specification Review
- Preliminary Design Review
- Critical Design Review
- Test Readiness Review
- Functional Configuration Audit
- Physical Configuration Audit
- Formal Qualification Review

The reviews required by MIL-STD-1521B are summarized in Fig. B.4. Although these reviews and audits are required by and described briefly in DOD-STD-2167A, MIL-STD-1521B contains the detailed descriptions of formats and requirements along with checklists that will be used when conducting the reviews.

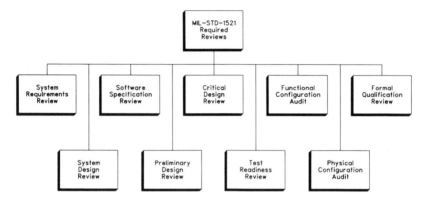

Figure B.4   Reviews Required by MIL-STD-1521

MIL-STD-483A.   MIL-STD-483A (Configuration Management Practices for Systems, Equipment, Munitions, and Computer Programs) is normally only invoked on contracts requiring concurrent software and hardware development. MIL-STD-483A requires slightly more stringent configuration management of the software development effort than that required in DOD-STD-2167A in that computer software configuration identification and configuration management records and reports are required.

Summary

Small to mid–sized software development projects normally will use DOD-STD-2167A with tailoring to combine required documents, eliminate unneeded documents, or eliminate unnecessary portions of documents. Review meetings normally will be conducted in accordance with DOD-STD-2167A guidelines, and also may be combined with each other.

Large software development projects usually are conducted to DOD-STD-2167A guidelines with all or most deliverables required in accordance with the DOD-STD-2167A DIDs. Review meetings normally are more formal, and are often conducted to MIL-STD-1521B specifications. Portions of the System Engineering Management Guide that are applicable to software development may be required or expected.

System projects normally are conducted to MIL-STD-490A requirements, with software developers also required to follow DOD-STD-2167A requirements. System projects virtually always conduct reviews in accordance with MIL-STD-1521B, and software developers should be prepared to meet all software-related requirements in that document. System projects normally are conducted in accordance with the guidelines in the System Engineering Management Guide, so knowledge of this manual is required. If configuration management is expected to be a problem, the configuration management guidelines in MIL-STD-483 may be required, although tailoring in the software area is often allowed.

B.2 MILITARY SYSTEM HIERARCHIES

Figure B.5 summarizes how the military decomposes systems into organized hierarchies. At the system and segment levels, we are dealing with entities that generally are a combination of software and

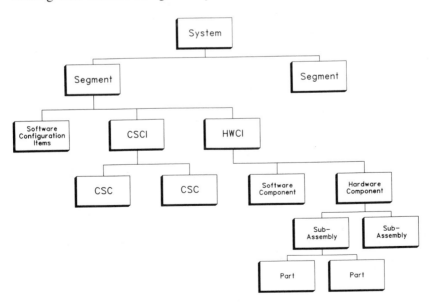

Figure B.5   Military System Decomposition

hardware. A system is a collection of hardware, software, material, facilities, personnel, data, and services required to perform a designated function with specified results. A segment is a grouping of elements from the system that are closely related and often physically interfaced. For example, we describe the command and control system on board a Navy ship. The command and control system consists of components that work together to accomplish a common mission, rely on each other for some data, but can be developed and tested independently. Within the command and control system, a dedicated computer and software program for command and control processing (the C^2P) might be one segment, the Afloat Correlation System (ACS) might be a second segment, the JTIDS/LINK-16 terminal a third, etc.

Each segment consists of some combination of hardware configuration items (HWCIs), computer software configuration items (CSCIs), and software configuration items (SCIs). Each configuration item normally is responsible for a single top-level function, and usually is developed by one prime contractor. These three types of configuration items are defined as follows:

- *Hardware configuration items* (HWCIs) are hardware and/or firmware system segment components. They will be developed or integrated together to form the hardware portion of a system. HWCIs are classified into prime items (complex, critical components), critical items (noncomplex, critical components), noncomplex items (noncomplex, noncritical components), and facilities or ships (see Fig. B.6 for a summary).

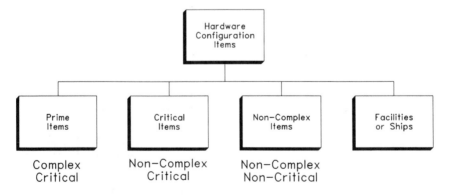

Figure B.6   Types of Hardware Configuration Items

- *Computer software configuration items* (CSCIs), also called category one software configuration items, are deliverable software that is to be developed specifically for the system in question.
- *Software configuration items* refer to software in the following categories: nondeliverable software used during development (category 3); unmodified commercially available software (category 4); or previously developed software (category 5). Category 2 software refers to embedded software, which is discussed below.

As much as possible, the system should be decomposed into configuration items that allow parallel development and testing (that is, as few dependencies *between* configuration items as possible).

Computer software configuration items (CSCIs) are decomposed into Computer Software Components (CSCs), which are further decomposed into Computer Software Units (CSUs). Hardware configuration items (HWCIs) consist of hardware components and software components. Software components are embedded software, which are classified as category 2 software. Hardware components can be further divided into subassemblies and parts. Figure B.7 illustrates the hierarchical decomposition of military systems.

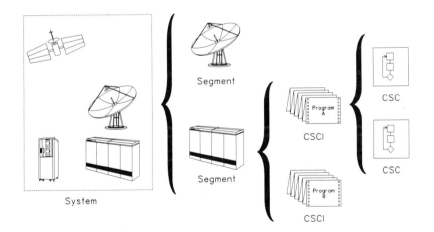

Figure B.7   Hierarchical Decomposition of Military Systems

B.3 CATEGORIES OF MILITARY SOFTWARE

As mentioned in the previous section, military software configuration items are divided into one of five categories. Category 1 software is defined as deliverable software to be developed and designated as a computer software configuration item (CSCI). Some of the factors used to decide if software should be designated as a CSCI are

- Functional complexity of the software
- Estimated size and criticality of the program
- Interface, data base, and integration complexity
- Complexity of security requirements
- Certification requirements
- Probability of change during the development cycle
- Operational criticality of the software
- Development location(s)
- Schedule

Developed software that is embedded in hardware can be classified as either a category 1 or category 2 configuration item. Category 2 configuration items are defined as deliverable software to be developed and designated as part of a system or hardware configuration item. Designating software as category 2 typically imposes fewer documentation requirements than category 1 on the software developer. The primary factors that determine if embedded software can be treated as category 2 are

- Size
- Complexity
- Probability of change
- Intended end use

During most large software development projects, some software will be developed that is used for testing, verification, prototyping, and so on and that is not intended for delivery. Nondeliverable software used during the development effort is called category 3 software. This software is still subject to some control under DOD-STD-2167A, but the control is all focused on ensuring that the category 3 software functions properly (that is, gives valid answers) when used during development.

Unmodified commercially available software that is used in a CSCI or HWCI is considered category 4 software. It should be stressed that you must be careful to receive the permission of the government contracting officer to use commercial software (including the operating system and utilities, data base management system, etc.) in any military system. The government is concerned that future changes to (or unavailability of) the commercial software will render their program unmaintainable and useless. With the possible exception of the operating system and utilities, the government normally would rather have full rights, including source code, to all programs in a military system.

Previously developed computer programs that are to be re-used with or without modifications are considered category 5 software. We will see that category 5 documentation is no less stringent than category 1, but most documents should already exist and require modification at most.

B.4 MILITARY SOFTWARE DEVELOPMENT LIFE CYCLE

Figure B.8 shows the four phases of military systems development and procurement. The cycle is started when a mission need is identified, which might be based on input from the operational military, one of the Navy research facilities, or even from a private contractor. The concept exploration phase is initiated with the approval of the military program objective memorandum, and involves definition of system concepts for further development. Following successful completion of the concept exploration phase, the demonstration and validation phase is initiated, often with the assistance of private contractors. This phase includes preliminary design work, prototyping, and other activities necessary to determine if the project should proceed to full-scale development. Full-scale development involves the actual production of

Figure B.8   Four Phases of Military Systems Development

a product or program that can be evaluated in the field. Finally, successful completion of field-level testing signals the start of production and deployment of the product or program.

Figure B.9 shows how the various stages of software development fit into the phases of procurement. Figure B.10 adds the reviews that normally are conducted during this process. Note that the products of the system design review will be considered the system's functional baseline, the products of the software specification review will be considered the system's allocated baseline, and the products of the

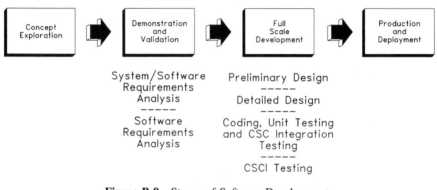

Figure B.9   Stages of Software Development

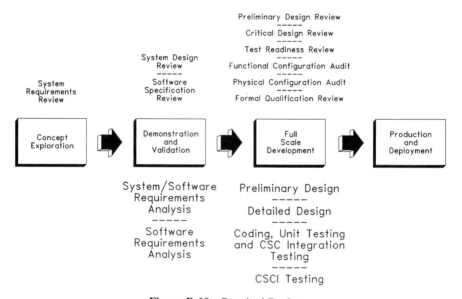

Figure B.10   Required Reviews

physical configuration audit will be considered the system's product baseline. Figure B.11 shows how the various components of structured software development fit into the phases of procurement. Figure B.12 shows the documents you may be tasked to produce, and the phase during which they are written and approved.

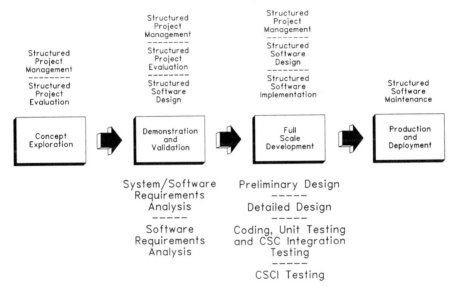

Figure B.11   Structured Software Development Life Cycle

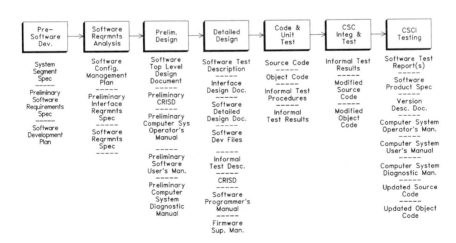

Figure B.12   DOD-STD-2167 Documents by Project Phase

B.5 MILITARY SOFTWARE DEVELOPMENT DEPENDENCIES

The nine reviews and audits required by DOD-STD-2167A and MIL-STD-1521B typically are considered milestone events when defining dependencies. As shown in Fig. B.13, the tasks typically conducted prior to the System Requirements Review are as follows (tasks with no software input are not shown):

- Mission and requirements analysis
- Functional flow analysis
- Preliminary requirements allocation
- System/cost effectiveness analysis
- Integrated test plan
- Hardware and software reliability analysis
- Hardware and software maintainability analysis
- System interface studies
- Program risk analysis
- Technical performance measurement planning
- Data management plans

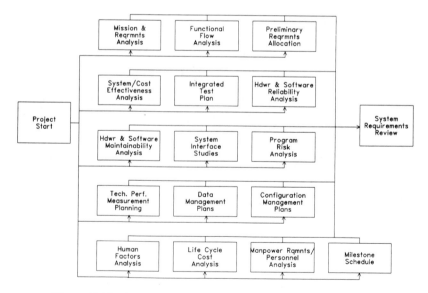

Figure B.13   Dependencies Prior to System Requirements Review

- Configuration management plans
- Human factors analysis
- Life cycle cost analysis
- Manpower requirements/personnel analysis
- Milestone schedule

These documents deal with the system or segment as a whole, and so will address both software and hardware issues. Many of these documents are combined into a single document with a chapter covering each area. Also, most of the documents produced at this stage have an informal format, often consisting of no more than one to five pages of information.

After successful completion of the System Requirements Review (SRR), work begins to prepare for the System Design Review (SDR). As shown in Fig. B.14, the following documents normally are produced after the SRR but prior to the SDR:

- System or Segment (as appropriate) Specification (Type A specification)
- System or Segment (as appropriate) Design Document
- System cost estimates
- Preliminary Operational Concept Document
- Preliminary Interface Requirements Specification
- Preliminary Software Requirements Specification
- Preliminary Software Development Specification (Type B5 specification)

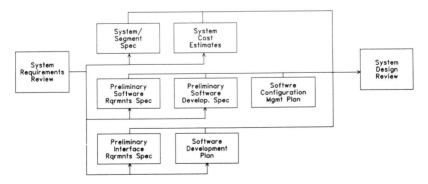

Figure B.14   Dependencies Prior to System Design Review

- Software Configuration Management Plan (if required)
- Software Quality Evaluation Plan (if required)
- Software Development Plan

Successful completion of the SDR results in a functional baseline for the system. This functional baseline describes the specific capabilities that the system must be designed to meet. Changes to these capabilities must be formally submitted as Engineering Change Proposals (ECPs), and must be approved by the government. Note that the functional baseline corresponds to the function-oriented plan described in this book, in which the design hierarchy includes function-oriented modules (menus, key-activated, interrupt) but no internal modules.

Unlike the SRR and SDR, which treat the system as a whole, the Software Specification Review (SSR) deals with a single software configuration item. If one SSR is held dealing with multiple configuration items simultaneously, they are still treated individually during the meeting.

Figure B.15 shows the dependency links between all tasks conducted after completion of the SDR and prior to the Software Specification Review. When dealing with existing software (category 5 configuration items), the documents simply may be revised or updated versions of materials used during the original development. In

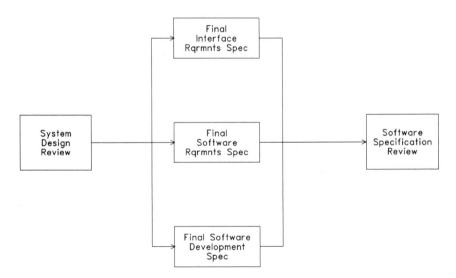

Figure B.15   Dependencies Prior to Software Specification Review

summary, the documents that are produced after the SDR in preparation for the SRR are

- Final Operational Concept Document
- Final Interface Requirements Specification
- Final Software Requirements Specification
- Final Software Development Specification (Type B5 specification)

After successful completion of the Software Specification Review, the system functional requirements allocations are frozen as the allocated baseline for use during design. Once again, changes to the allocated baseline after this point will require Engineering Change Proposals that must be approved by the government.

A Preliminary Design Review is conducted for each software configuration item, or for a group of functionally related configuration items. As shown in Fig. B.16, the following documents are produced in preparation for the Preliminary Design Review (PDR):

- Preliminary Computer Resources Integrated Support Document
- Preliminary Computer System Operator's Manual
- Preliminary Software User's Manual
- Preliminary Computer System Diagnostic Manual

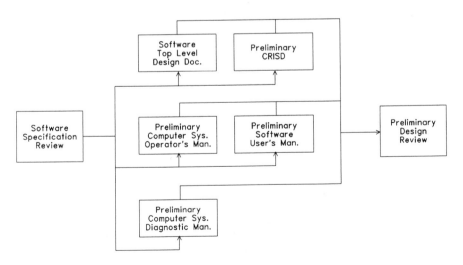

Figure B.16   Dependencies Prior to Preliminary Design Review

After completion of a Preliminary Design Review for each configuration item (or a combined review), detailed software design work can begin. This detailed design work will culminate in a Critical Design Review (CDR) for each configuration item, as well as a CDR for the system as a whole. It is at this point that the design has been fleshed out to include internal modules (process, common, and library) and their descriptions. As shown in Fig. B.17, the following documents are produced when preparing for the CDR:

- Software Test Description
- Interface Design Document
- Software Design Document
- Final Computer Resources Integrated Support Document
- Software Programmer's Manual
- Firmware Support Manual

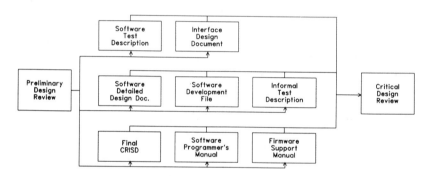

Figure B.17   Dependencies Prior to Critical Design Review

Following completion of the CDR, detailed coding and integration can begin. During the coding and integration stage, the following documents are produced (see Fig. B.18):

- Source code
- Object code

Finally, as shown in Fig. B.19, the software is integrated into the system and prepared for the Functional Configuration Audit and Physical Configuration Audit. During this time, the following documents are produced:

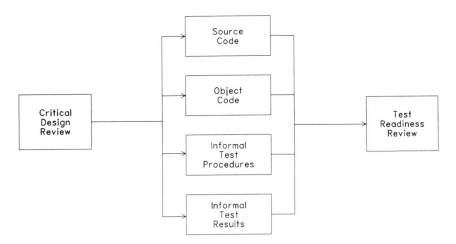

Figure B.18   Dependencies Prior to Test Readiness Review

- Software Test Reports
- Software Product Specification (Type C5 specification)
- Version Description Document
- Final Software User's Manual
- Final Computer System Diagnostic Manual
- Final version of source code
- Final version of object code

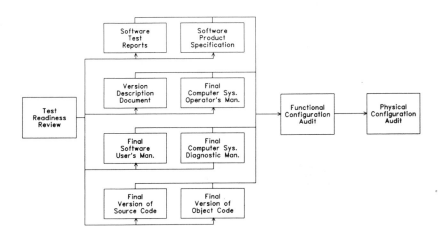

Figure B.19   Dependencies Prior to Configuration Audits

B.6 MILITARY SOFTWARE DOCUMENTATION REQUIREMENTS

Tables B1–B6 show all software and system-related documentation and review requirements for large military development projects. Across the top of the tables, you will find the various hierarchical elements in a military system. The table shows, for each type of hierarchical element, which documents must be produced. For example, the table shows that the Computer System Operator's Manual applies to a segment. This means that an individual version of this document normally does not need to be produced for each software configuration item. On the other hand, the table shows that each category 1 software configuration item (CSCI) requires a software Requirements Specification. This means that a version of the Software Requirements Specification must be produced for *each* CSCI in the system/segment. I have also included a reference to one or more military standards for each document or review.

HIPO-II is designed to produce program documentation that is compatible with the requirements of many of the government's Data Item Deliverables (DIDs). For each appropriate document, we will describe the relationship between HIPO-II design documentation and the appropriate DID requirements. It will be assumed that the project team is using the integrated tools *Structured Project Manager's Toolbox* and *Structured Designer's Toolbox* to perform the work.

Mission and Requirements Analysis. This unstructured report describes the basic requirements that the software is expected to meet. This requirement can be met by a statement of need plus a prototype of the system processing generated using the HIPO-II techniques described in this book. An end user and systems analyst can work together to quickly put together a hierarchy of menu choices and interrupt/keyboard capabilities. A few sample screens and reports can be added to clarify functions when necessary. Processing descriptions for these functional modules should be high level, loosely structured, and should be traceable back to the statement of need. This prototype and the accompanying statement of need then become the requirements document.

Functional Flow Analysis. For each of the functional modules just identified, input and output variables can be identified. The

	System	Segment	HWCI	CSCI (Cat 1)	SW Comp (Cat 2)	Non-Del Sw (Cat 3)	SWCI (Cat 4)	Prev Dev SW (Cat 5)	Required By
System Rqrmnts Review	✓	✓							MIL−STD−1521 DOD−STD−2167
System Design Review	✓	✓							MIL−STD−1521 DOD−STD−2167
Software Specification Review				✓	✓			✓	MIL−STD−1521 DOD−STD−2167
Preliminary Design Review			✓	✓	✓			✓	MIL−STD−1521 DOD−STD−2167
Critical Design Review			✓	✓	✓			✓	MIL−STD−1521 DOD−STD−2167
Test Readiness Review				✓	✓			✓	MIL−STD−1521 DOD−STD−2167
Functional Configuration Audit			✓	✓	✓			✓	MIL−STD−1521 DOD−STD−2167
Physical Configuration Audit			✓	✓	✓	✓		✓	MIL−STD−1521 DOD−STD−2167
Formal Qualification Review			✓	✓	✓			✓	MIL−STD−1521 DOD−STD−2167

Table B.1

functional program hierarchy and accompanying IPO charts now become the functional flow analysis.

Preliminary Requirements Allocation. The functional program hierarchy and accompanying processing descriptions form the basis for a preliminary requirements allocation. If timing or storage is critical, CPU cycles or storage space might be allocated to individual modules during this process.

System/Cost-Effectiveness Analysis. The program hierarchy can be downloaded into Structured Project Manager's Toolbox

	System	Segment	HWCI	CSCI (Cat 1)	SW Comp (Cat 2)	Non-Del Sw (Cat 3)	SWCI (Cat 4)	Prev Dev SW (Cat 5)	Required By
Mission & Rqrmnts Analysis	✓	✓							MIL-STD-1521
Functional Flow Analysis	✓	✓							MIL-STD-1521
Preliminary Requirements Allocation	✓	✓							MIL-STD-1521
System/Cost Effectiveness Analysis	✓	✓							MIL-STD-1521
Integrated Test Plan	✓	✓							MIL-STD-1521
Hdwr & SW Reliability Analysis	✓	✓							MIL-STD-1521
Hdwr & SW Maint. Analysis	✓	✓							MIL-STD-1521
System Interface Studies	✓	✓							MIL-STD-1521
Program Risk Analysis	✓	✓							MIL-STD-1521

Table B.2

(SPMT) for costing. The resulting cost estimates must be matched against expected benefits.

Integrated Test Plan. SPMT normally will include a project work breakdown structure that includes software, hardware, and integration-related tasks. The scheduling capabilities of SPMT should be used to plan for and schedule integration activities.

Hardware and Software Reliability Analysis. From within SPMT, specific reliability requirements can be allocated to top-level components (HWCIs and CSCIs).

	System	Segment	HWCI	CSCI (Cat 1)	SW Comp (Cat 2)	Non-Del Sw (Cat 3)	SWCI (Cat 4)	Prev Dev SW (Cat 5)	Required By
Tech. Perf. Measurement Planning	✓	✓							MIL–STD–1521
Data Management Plans	✓	✓							MIL–STD–1521
Configuration Management Plan	✓	✓							MIL–STD–1521
Human Factors Analysis	✓	✓							MIL–STD–1521
Life Cycle Cost Analysis	✓	✓							MIL–STD–1521
Manpower Requirements Analysis	✓	✓							MIL–STD–1521
Milestone Schedule	✓	✓							MIL–STD–1521
Type A System/ Segment Spec	✓	✓							MIL–STD–490 DOD–STD–2167
Type B Development Spec			✓	✓				✓	MIL–STD–490

Table B.3

Hardware and Software Maintainability Analysis.   When generating a program hierarchy, the structure should be designed to facilitate maintainability. The logic used during this process and program structure arrived at is written down as the software maintainability analysis.

Program Risk Analysis.   The risk analysis and ranking capabilities of SPMT can be applied to the project tasks, including software hierarchy modules.

Technical Performance Measurement Planning.   The modules identified in the program hierarchy can be required, in their

	System	Segment	HWCI	CSCI (Cat 1)	SW Comp (Cat 2)	Non-Del Sw (Cat 3)	SWCI (Cat 4)	Prev Dev SW (Cat 5)	Required By
Type C Product Spec			✓	✓				✓	MIL–STD–490
Type D Process Spec			✓						MIL–STD–490
Type E Material Spec			✓						MIL–STD–490
Software Development Plan				✓					DOD–STD–2167
Interface Requirements Spec				✓	✓			✓	DOD–STD–2167
Software Product Spec				✓	✓			✓	DOD–STD–2167
Software Requirements Spec				✓	✓			✓	DOD–STD–2167

Table B.4

header description, to meet certain performance requirements. Performance requirements for reliability, precision, timing, and storage are some areas that often are critical and thus might be appropriate for allocation.

Configuration Management Plan. The ability of SDT to maintain the program documentation on-line greatly simplifies configuration management (problems of programmers using out-of-date documentation). A procedure should be established to restrict changes to the on-line documentation to an individual or group to prevent improper changes.

	System	Segment	HWCI	CSCI (Cat 1)	SW Comp (Cat 2)	Non-Del Sw (Cat 3)	SWCI (Cat 4)	Prev Dev SW (Cat 5)	Required By
Configuration Management Plan			✓	✓	✓	✓		✓	MIL-STD-483
Software Top Level Design Doc.				✓	✓			✓	DOD-STD-2167
Software Detailed Design Doc.				✓	✓			✓	DOD-STD-2167
Interface Design Document				✓	✓			✓	DOD-STD-2167
Software Test Description				✓		✓		✓	DOD-STD-2167
Version Description Document				✓	✓			✓	DOD-STD-2167

Table B.5

Human Factors Analysis. As more sample outputs are added to the design, the SDT prototype and user feedback from its use become the human factors analysis.

Life Cycle Cost Analysis. SPMT includes life cycle cost analysis capabilities by including tasks related to maintenance and support.

Manpower Requirements Analysis. SPMT includes resource requirement reports, including manpower requirements.

	System	Segment	HWCI	CSCI (Cat 1)	SW Comp (Cat 2)	Non-Del Sw (Cat 3)	SWCI (Cat 4)	Prev Dev SW (Cat 5)	Required By
Software Test Report				✓		✓		✓	DOD–STD–2167
Test & Evaluation Master Plan	✓	✓							DODD–5000.3
Computer Sys. Operator's Manual		✓							DOD–STD–2167
Software User's Manual		✓							DOD–STD–2167
Computer Sys. Diagnostic Manual		✓							DOD–STD–2167
Software Programmer's Manual		✓							DOD–STD–2167
Firmware Support Manual						✓			DOD–STD–2167
CRISD		✓							DOD–STD–2167

Table B.6

Milestone Schedule.   SPMT supports scheduling in general, and milestone scheduling in particular.

System/Segment Design Document.   This report uses the system hierarchy (maintained by SPMT) plus IPO definitions for software modules (from SDT).

Software Development Plan.   This report presents the complete software development plan, including resource requirements and schedule. This report will include many of the SPMT outputs, including task definitions, resource estimates, dependency definitions, and schedules.

Software Requirements Specification.   This can be prepared using Input-Process-Output charts and data hierarchy charts. Processing descriptions for some top-level modules can use decision table format. Description line for data elements can specify required information for scaling, conventions, and content.

Interface Requirements Specification.   The input-output definitions for software modules indicate any modules receiving input from external hardware. These interfaces must be defined in this document.

Software Product Specification.   This document consists of the program hierarchy (top-level detail and all detail), data hierarchy, IPO charts, and source code.

Configuration Management Plan.   The fact that design documentation is maintained online simplifies preparation of the configuration management plan and procedures.

Software Design Document.   The program and data hierarchy, module header information, and module processing descriptions meet the requirements for program structure and algorithm description in this document.

Software Test Description.   The functional portion of the program hierarchy (menu, interrupt, and keyboard modules) identifies natural test points for threaded (depth first) top-down testing.

Software User's Manual.   The prototyping capabilities of HIPO-II facilitate early work on this document. The sample outputs used during prototyping can be incorporated in the Software User's Manual.

BIBLIOGRAPHY

Ada Training Curriculum, report AD-A165-302. Softech, Inc., 1986.

Bergland, G., and R. Gordon, *Software Design Strategies.* IEEE Computer Society, 1981.

Cleland, D., *Systems Analysis and Project Management.* New York, NY: McGraw-Hill Book Company, 1983.

DeMarco, T., *Structured Analysis and System Specification.* Yourdon Press, 1979.

Deutsch, M., *Software Verification and Validation.* Englewood Cliffs, NJ: Prentice Hall, Inc., 1982.

Dijkstra, E., "Notes on Structured Programming," in *Structured Programming.* New York, NY: Academic Press, 1972.

Freeman, P., and A. Wasserman (ed.), *Tutorial on Software Design Techniques.* IEEE Computer Society, 1983.

Gilbert, P., *Software Design and Development.* Chicago, IL: Science Research Associates, Inc., 1983.

Higgins, D., *Designing Structured Programs.* Englewood Cliffs, NJ: Prentice Hall, Inc., 1983.

Higgins, D., *Program Design and Construction.* Englewood Cliffs, NJ: Prentice Hall, Inc., 1979.

IBM, IBM HIPO, *A Design Aid and Documentation Technique,* 6C20–185D. White Plains, NY: IBM Corporation. 1974.

Jensen, R., and C. Tonies, *Software Engineering.* Englewood Cliffs, NJ: Prentice Hall, Inc., 1979.

Martin, J., and C. McClure, *Software Maintenance, the Problem and its Solutions.* Englewood Cliffs, NJ: Prentice Hall, Inc., 1983.

Martin, J., and C. McClure, *Action Diagrams.* Englewood Cliffs, NJ: Prentice Hall, Inc., 1985.

Martin, J., and C. McClure, *Diagramming Techniques for Analysts and Programmers.* Englewood Cliffs, NJ: Prentice Hall, Inc., 1985.

Martin, J., and C. McClure, *Structured Techniques for Computing.* Englewood Cliffs, NJ: Prentice-Hall, Inc., 1985.

Martin, J., *Systems Design from Provably Correct Constructs*. Englewood Cliffs, NJ: Prentice Hall, Inc., 1979.

Mills, H., *Debugging Techniques in Larger Systems,* ed. R. Rustin. Englewood Cliffs, NJ: Prentice Hall, Inc., 1971.

Mills, H., *Software Productivity*. Boston, MA: Little, Brown and Co., 1983.

Orr, K., *Structured Systems Development*. Yourdon Press, 1977.

Orr, K., *Structured Requirements Definition*. Ken Orr and Associates, 1981.

Parnas, D., *Information Distribution Aspects of Design Methodology*. Pittsburgh, Pa: Technical Report, Department of Computer Science, Carnegie-Mellon University, 1971.

Parnas, D., "On the Criteria to be Used in Decomposing Systems into Modules," *Communications of the ACM,* pp. 1053-58, December, 1972.

Rader, R., *Advanced Software Design Techniques*. Petrocelli, 1978.

Ramsey, H., M. Atwood, and J. Van Doren, *A Comparative Study of Flowcharts and Program Design Languages for Detailed Procedural Specification of Computer Programs,* Technical Report #SAI-78-78- DEN. Science Applications, Inc., 1978.

Roetzheim, W., *Proposal Writing for the Data Processing Consultant*. Englewood Cliffs, NJ: Prentice Hall, Inc., 1986.

Roetzheim, W., *Structured Computer Project Management*. Englewood Cliffs, NJ: Prentice Hall, Inc., 1988.

Sheppard, S., E. Kruesi, and B. Curtis. *The Effects of Symbology and Spatial Arrangement on the Comprehension of Software Specifications,* Report TR-80-388200-2. General Electric, October, 1980.

Shevlin, J., *"Evaluating Alternative Methods of Systems Analysis,"* *Data Management,* pp. 22-25, April 1983.

Shneiderman, B., B. Mayer, et.al., *Experimental Investigations on the Utility of Detailed Flowcharts in Programming,* vol. 20, 373-81. Communications of the ACM, 1977.

Sime, M., B. Mayer, et. al., "Structuring the Programmer's Task," *Journal of Occupational Psychology,* vol. 50, 205-16, 1977.

Sneed, H., *Software Renewal: A Case Study*. IEEE Software, July 1984, pp. 56-63.

Weinberg, V., *Structured Analysis*. Englewood Cliffs, NJ: Prentice Hall, Inc., 1979.

Wirth, N., "On the Composition of Well-Structured Programs," *Computing Surveys, 6, No. 4, December, 1974*.

Yourdon, E., and L. Constantine, *Structured Design*. Yourdon Press, 1986.

Yourdon, E., *Managing the Structured Techniques*. Yourdon Press, 1986.

INDEX

Yes! Rush me a copy of *Structured Designer's Toolbox* (SDT) so I can begin applying the theories in this book to actual projects. I understand that SDT runs on an IBM PC or compatible, and requires 512 Kbytes of memory.

Name: _____

Address: _____

Address: _____

City: _____ State: _____ Zip: _____

Phone: (_____) _____

Please send _____ copies of SDT at $492 each: $ _____

U.S. shipping at $6 per copy: _____

Optional 2nd day air shipping at $9 per copy: _____

International Shipping at $12 per copy: _____

CA residents, add 7% sales tax: _____

Total due: $ _____

_____ Please ship to me UPS Cash On Delivery (COD). I will pay with a check on delivery (U.S. only).

_____ I have enclosed a check for the total amount due. Please ship my order UPS prepaid.

NOTE: We cannot invoice you for copies of SDT. All shipments must be UPS, COD or prepaid.

COD Phone orders are accepted, or return a copy of this form to:

William H. Roetzheim & Associates
3891 American Avenue
La Mesa, CA 92041
(619) 464-0182

5200   6990